Retirement Insecurity

Other books and studies from the

ECONOMIC POLICY INSTITUTE

The State of Working America

Hardships in America
The Real Story of Working Families

Shared Work, Valued Care
New Norms for Organizing Market Work and Unpaid Care Work

How Much Is Enough?
Basic Family Budgets for Working Families

The Class Size Debate

Manufacturing Advantage
Why High Performance Work Systems Pay Off

*Economic Policy Institute books are available in bookstores
and at www.epinet.org*

Retirement Insecurity

The Income Shortfalls Awaiting the Soon-to-Retire

Edward N. Wolff

Economic Policy Institute

This research and its publication were supported by a grant
from The Retirement Research Foundation.

ISBN: 1-932066-01-2

Contents

About the Author

Edward N. Wolff is professor of economics at New York University, where he has taught since 1974. He is also managing editor of the *Review of Income and Wealth*, a senior scholar at the Levy Economics Institute of Bard College, a research associate at the National Bureau of Economic Research, and president of the Eastern Economics Association. He also serves as a council member of the International Input-Output Association, is a past council member of the International Association for Research in Income and Wealth, and has acted as a consultant with the Economic Policy Institute, the World Bank, the United Nations, and the WIDER Institute. His principal research areas are productivity growth and income and wealth distribution. He is the author (or co-author) of *Growth, Accumulation, and Unproductive Activity* (1987); *Productivity and American Leadership* (1989); *Competitiveness, Convergence, and International Specialization* (1993); and *Top Heavy: A Study of Increasing Inequality of Wealth in America* (2002). He received his Ph.D. from Yale University in 1974.

I. Introduction

Today's older workers will live longer and spend more time in retirement than workers in any previous generation. This trend presents a challenge to workers and to public policy that has to date been met with analyses that, by looking primarily at household wealth and savings, address the issue only around the edges. The key question, however, tends to be ignored: will households have enough *income* to afford a decent standard of living in retirement?

Between 1989 and 1998, a period of strong economic growth and a 248% rise in stock prices, the annual income that a household headed by a person approaching retirement (i.e., age 47-64) could expect in retirement rose at the average by 7%, to $50,000 a year. But gains for the average have not meant gains for all households. Over this same period, the share of these near-retirement households unable to expect adequate income in retirement increased:

- By 1998 (the latest year of available data), 18.5% of households headed by a person approaching retirement could expect incomes below the poverty line. This share actually increased during the 1990s, up from 17.2% in 1989.

- The share of these households unable to replace half of their pre-retirement income rose sharply, from 29.9% in 1989 to 42.5% in 1998. The share was even higher in 1998 among African American and Hispanic households, at 52.7%.

The increasing reliance on individual investment of retirement funds – exemplified most clearly by the growth in 401(k)s, individual retirement accounts, and other defined contribution pension plans – and the decline in traditional pensions, might lead one to expect that the period of fast stock market growth that began in 1983 would have produced more retirement wealth and improved retirement income adequacy. After all, by 1998 59.7% of households approaching retirement had investments in defined contribution accounts, up from 11.9% in 1983.

Yet for the typical (median) household headed by a person age 47-64, retirement wealth actually declined from 1983 to 1998, by 11%, while rising 4% on average. Retirement wealth declined for the household at the middle of the wealth distribution while it rose overall because the pattern of retirement wealth growth was very unequal:

- Among households headed by a person approaching retirement, only households with wealth holdings above $1 million saw consistent increases in their wealth, after inflation. All other wealth classes, even those with between $500,000 and $1 million in net worth, saw their retirement wealth fall from 1983 to 1998.

- Growth in retirement wealth tended to be the province of white households, who saw a 6.1% increase in average retirement wealth. Black and Hispanic households experienced a 19.9% drop.

- Growth in retirement wealth also tended to be the province of college-educated households, who experienced a 6.4% increase in their average wealth. Among the 72% of the workforce without a college degree, mean retirement wealth dropped by 39.1% where the household head had less than 12 years of schooling, 9.9% for high school graduates, and 10.5% for workers with some college.

One reason for the deterioration of retirement wealth for the typical household is that pension coverage for households (either traditional pension or defined contribution plan) barely changed from 1983 to 1998. Among households headed by a person age 47-64, 73.7% were covered by a pension plan in 1998, an improvement of only 3.5 percentage points in pension coverage compared to 1983. At this rate it will take 113 years to achieve pension coverage for all households.

Thus, an extraordinary 15-year run-up in stock prices at a time when public policy was encouraging expanded individual investment for retirement did not enhance retirement income adequacy for the typical household, even as the market was near its height. Moreover, it is important to remember that all gains made after 1998 in terms of household wealth had disappeared by the third quarter of 2001, when household financial net worth fell back to its third-quarter 1998 level. New policies are needed to ensure that the broad majority of households have access to pensions and adequate incomes in retirement.

As a first step for public policy, pension coverage needs to be improved. Until then, as long as a substantial share of future retirees lack adequate resources, it seems prudent for policy makers to keep Social Security intact, rather than subject it to the risks of privatization. This is particularly true now that Social Security offers almost universal coverage: thanks to mandatory coverage for most workers, Social Security's reach rose from 82.4% in 1983 to 98.4% in 1998.

Next, retirement wealth accumulation needs to be improved for the vast majority of households. The growing system of voluntary accounts in the United States has produced greater inequality between rich and median households and declining retirement wealth for the typical household. In contrast, Social Security, which pools contributions in order to ensure a retirement income floor for all participants, is the one segment of the retirement system that distributes its wealth universally. Thus, one possibility for improving the adequacy of retirement income for the typical household would be to improve Social Security benefits.

II. Measures of wealth, retirement wealth, and retirement income adequacy

This evaluation of changes in retirement income adequacy over the past two decades proceeds in three steps. The first is a calculation of how much wealth – in its various manifestations, including marketable wealth, pension wealth, and Social Security wealth – households held in 1998 and how that amount changed compared to 1989 and 1983. The second step is a calculation of the stream of retirement income that today's older workers can expect from their accumulated wealth at the time of their retirement. The last step is a comparison of the expected income stream generated from different wealth holdings to two standards of adequate retirement income: a poverty level income, and the ratio of final earnings replaced by retirement income. These measures allow an assessment of the adequacy of projected retirement incomes and an evaluation of how adequacy has changed over time.

One of the most important and also consistent findings in the literature is that wealth dispersion is unequal. Consequently, this analysis studies the changes in wealth and retirement income security for households with different demographic characteristics, such as age, gender, race or ethnicity, education, marital status, and homeownership status.

The starting point of the analysis is to measure total wealth (termed here "augmented wealth"), which combines three dimensions of wealth computed from Survey of Consumer Finance (SCF) data: marketable wealth, defined benefit pension wealth, and Social Security wealth. This concept is illustrated in **Figure A**.

Marketable wealth (or net worth) is defined as the current value of all marketable or fungible assets less the current value of debts. Net worth is thus the difference in value between total assets and total liabilities. Total assets are defined as the sum of: (1) the gross value of owner-occupied housing; (2) other real estate owned by the household; (3) cash and demand deposits; (4) time and savings deposits, certificates of deposit, and money market accounts; (5) government bonds, corporate bonds, foreign bonds, and other financial securities; (6) the cash surrender value of life insurance plans; (7) the cash surrender value of pension plans, including individual retirement accounts (IRAs), Keoghs, and 401(k) plans; (8) corporate stock and mutual funds; (9) net equity in unincorporated businesses; and (10) equity in trust funds. Total liabilities are the sum of: (1) mortgage debt, (2) consumer debt, including auto loans, and (3) other debt.

This measure reflects wealth as a store of value and therefore a source of

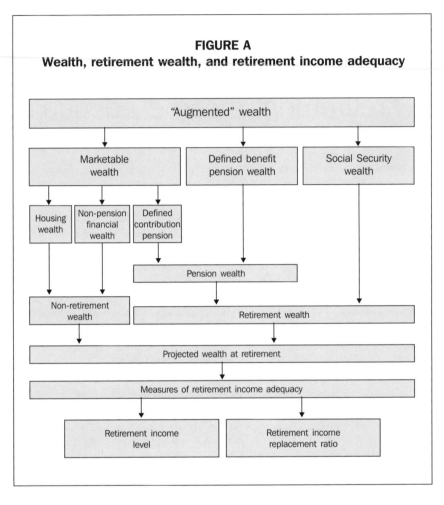

FIGURE A
Wealth, retirement wealth, and retirement income adequacy

potential consumption. The assumption is that this concept best reflects the level of well being associated with a family's holdings. Thus, only assets that can be readily converted to cash (that is, "fungible" ones) are included. As a result, consumer durables, such as automobiles, televisions, furniture, household appliances, and the like, are excluded here, since these items are not easily marketed or their resale value typically far understates the value of their consumption services to the household.

This analysis includes some data on a more restricted concept of wealth, referred to here as "financial wealth," defined as net worth minus net equity in owner-occupied housing. Financial wealth is a more "liquid" concept than marketable wealth, since one's home is difficult to convert into cash in the short term. It thus reflects the resources that may be immediately available for consumption or various forms of investments.

The imputation of both pension and Social Security wealth involves a large number of steps, which are detailed in the appendix. Pension wealth consists of two parts. The first is the value of defined contribution wealth, which is equal to the cash surrender value (or the value for which the assets could be sold at a given point in time) of pension plans, including IRAs, Keoghs, and 401(k) plans (included in the measure of marketable wealth, as discussed above). The second is the capitalized value of expected benefits from defined benefit pension plans. Social Security wealth is defined as the present value of expected future Social Security benefits.

These measures allow a computation of each of the three legs of the retirement stool, as shown in Figure A: pension wealth, Social Security wealth, and non-retirement wealth (marketable wealth less defined contribution pension wealth).

Total retirement wealth is subsequently used as the basis for calculations here for retirement income and several measures of retirement adequacy. Each retirement wealth component offers the household a separate stream of income. The sum of these income streams can then be compared to standards of retirement income adequacy, specifically, the poverty line and the household's total earnings in the year prior to retirement.

This study documents what has happened to each of the three resource components – pensions, other forms of marketable wealth, and Social Security – for older workers and retirees from 1983 to 1998. In particular, calculations are performed for age groups near retirement age, defined as workers between the ages of 47 and 64, specifically for the years 1983, 1989, and 1998.

The data sources used for this study are the 1983, 1989, 1992, 1995, and 1998 SCF, conducted by the Federal Reserve Board. Each survey consists of a core representative sample combined with a high-income supplement. The supplement is drawn from the Internal Revenue Service's Statistics of Income data file. For the 1983 SCF, for example, an income cut-off of $100,000 of adjusted gross income is the criterion for inclusion in the supplemental sample. The advantage of the high-income supplement is that it provides a much richer sample of high-income and, therefore, potentially very wealthy families.

III. Trends in Wealth, Income, and Retirement Security

Introduction

The incomes and wealth of older workers – those between the ages of 47 and 64 – have risen markedly from 1983 to 1998. Income grew on average by 20.4%, and mean augmented wealth (the sum of net worth and retirement wealth) grew by 8.8%, from $571,000 in 1983 to $619,000 in 1998 (**Table 1**).

A closer look reveals a shift in the composition of wealth. While the wealth held in traditional defined benefit plans declined, the wealth in defined contribution plans grew from 1983 to 1998. Defined benefit pension wealth for households between the ages of 47 and 64 declined by 39.4%, from $87,000 in 1983 to $52,700 in 1998. The most important explanation for this phenomenon is that the share of households in this age group covered by a defined benefit plan fell by 27 percentage points.

As the coverage by and the wealth accumulated in traditional defined benefit plans fell, the wealth held by households in defined contribution plans skyrocketed, on average. The average wealth held by households between the ages of 47 and 64 in defined contribution plans grew by 838.1% to $69,200 between 1983 and 1998. To a large degree the explosive growth of defined contribution plans is explained by the fact that the share of households who have such plans grew from 11.9% in 1983 to 59.7% in 1998.

The rise of defined contribution pensions plans more than fully compensated for the loss of defined benefit plans over the 1983-98 period with respect to both wealth and coverage. Total pension wealth (the sum of defined benefit plus defined contribution wealth) increased on average by 29.1% in real terms between 1983 and 1998 among households between the ages of 47 and 64 (Table 1). Also, pension coverage on a household basis grew over the same period, with the share of households between the ages of 47 and 64 covered by either a defined benefit or a defined contribution pension plan rising from 72% in 1983 to 74% in 1998.

In contrast to private market wealth, Social Security wealth actually fell on average. For households ages 47-64, mean Social Security wealth fell by 13.4% from 1983 to 1998 while Social Security coverage grew: by 1998, 99% of households were covered by Social Security, up from 86% in 1983. Average Social Security wealth fell amid rising coverage because of decreasing lifetime earnings, which translate directly into smaller Social Security benefit accruals.

Still, mean retirement wealth (the sum of defined contribution accounts, defined benefit wealth, and Social Security wealth) increased by 4% over the 1983-

TABLE 1. Household income and wealth, age 47 and over, 1983, 1989, and 1998
(in thousands, 1998 dollars)

	1983	1989	1998	Percentage change		
				1983-89	1989-98	1983-98
A. All, age 47 and over						
1. Mean income	$48.2	$49.7	$56.0	3.2%	12.6%	16.2%
2. Mean net worth less DC pensions (HDWX)	338.2	357.2	365.5	5.6%	2.3%	8.1%
3. Mean DC + DB pension wealth	79.1	82.4	115.9	4.3%	40.7%	46.6%
4. Mean Social Security wealth	138.5	113.8	123.1	-17.9%	8.2%	-11.1%
5. Mean augmented wealth	555.8	553.4	604.6	-0.4%	9.2%	8.8%
6. Median income	27.9	28.4	32.4	1.9%	14.1%	16.3%
7. Median net worth less DC pensions (HDWX)	95.9	108.1	98.0	12.7%	-9.3%	2.2%
8. Median retirement wealth	184.2	143.3	171.6	-22.2%	19.7%	-6.9%
9. Median augmented wealth	327.1	285.4	298.1	-12.7%	4.4%	-8.9%
B. Ages 47-64						
1. Mean income	58.2	62.7	70.1	7.6%	11.9%	20.4%
2. Mean net worth less DC pensions (HDWX)	336.0	358.9	375.5	6.8%	4.6%	11.7%
3. Mean DC + DB pension wealth	94.4	87.0	121.9	-7.8%	40.1%	29.1%

4. Mean Social Security wealth	140.6	106.2	121.7	-24.5%	14.6%	-13.4%
5. Mean augmented wealth	571.0	552.1	619.0	-3.3%	12.1%	8.4%
6. Median income	38.6	39.4	44.0	2.3%	11.6%	14.1%
7. Median net worth less DC pensions (HDWX)	98.6	113.6	82.1	15.2%	-27.8%	-16.8%
8. Median retirement wealth	196.8	140.0	175.2	-28.8%	25.1%	-11.0%
9. Median augmented wealth	348.8	288.8	290.6	-17.2%	0.6%	-16.7%
C. Ages 65 and over						
1. Mean income	33.9	34.4	37.6	1.7%	9.3%	11.2%
2. Mean net worth less DC pensions (HDWX)	341.3	355.2	352.6	4.1%	-0.7%	3.3%
3. Mean DC + DB pension wealth	57.4	77.1	108.3	34.3%	40.5%	88.7%
4. Mean Social Security wealth	135.6	122.7	125.0	-9.5%	1.9%	-7.8%
5. Mean augmented wealth	534.2	554.9	585.8	3.9%	5.6%	9.7%
6. Median income	17.8	18.9	21.0	6.6%	10.9%	18.3%
7. Median net worth less DC pensions (HDWX)	93.4	100.7	125.1	7.9%	24.2%	34.0%
8. Median retirement wealth	163.3	151.0	169.8	-7.5%	12.5%	4.0%
9. Median augmented wealth	289.3	284.7	308.9	-1.6%	8.5%	6.8%

Note: Households are classified by the age of the head of household.
Key: Retirement wealth (RW) = DC pensions (PCSV) + DB pension wealth (PW) + Social Security wealth (SSW).
Augmented wealth = net worth less PCSV (HDWX) + retirement wealth (RW).

Source: Author's computations from the 1983, 1989, and 1998 Survey of Consumer Finances.

98 period among households age 47 and 64. Put differently, on average, the rise of defined contribution plans compensated for the loss of defined benefit pension wealth and Social Security wealth between 1983 and 1998.

Rise in average wealth reflects growing inequality

The story reads differently when we look at trends in median, as opposed to average, values. The median reflects the level of well being associated with the typical family (the one in the middle of the distribution). If average wealth is greater than median wealth, the wealth distribution is unequal. Similarly, if average wealth increases faster than median wealth, we observe a trend toward greater inequality.

Median retirement wealth fell by 11% between 1983 and 1998 for workers in the 47-64 age group, while average wealth rose by 4% (Table 8). Altogether, median augmented wealth fell by 16.7% for ages 47-64, while average augmented wealth grew by 8.4% (Table 1). The difference in the trends for mean and median wealth indicates that the distribution of wealth became increasingly unequal between 1983 and 1998, but that the inequality in total augmented wealth grew slightly faster than the disparity in retirement wealth.

Wealth inequality across groups persist, but some groups catch up

The trends in total wealth and retirement wealth vary by demographic group. Although whites still had substantially higher levels of wealth than African Americans or Hispanics in 1998, the latter groups saw larger gains in their total wealth. In 1998, non-Hispanic white households had about four times the net worth, twice the income, and twice the pension, Social Security, and retirement wealth of African American and Hispanic households (see Table 11, discussed in more detail below). However, black and Hispanic households generally saw greater percentage gains in their mean income and wealth than did non-Hispanic whites.

The picture is more mixed in terms of retirement wealth only. Indeed, average retirement wealth among white households ages 47-64 rose 6.1% over the 1983-98 period, compared to a 19.9% drop among African Americans and Hispanics (see Table 10 below). In other words, minorities caught up with respect to total wealth, but fell behind in terms of retirement security.

Different educational attainment also resulted in differences in income and wealth. Average income for those age 47-64 without a college degree (less than 16 years of schooling) fell from 1983 to 1998 (see Table 13 below); note that the non-college-educated make up the vast majority of households. However, incomes for households with college degrees rose from 1983 to 1998 by 2.8%. Similarly, mean net worth (marketable wealth) rose by 8.2% for college-educated households ages 47-64 from 1983 to

1998, while it grew more slowly or actually fell for everybody else. Also, total augmented wealth declined more slowly for the average college-educated household in the age group 47-64 from 1983 to 1998 than for anybody else.

Wealth also diverged by marital status, with married couples generally faring better than singles, and single men faring better than single women (see Tables 14 and 15 below). In 1998, the average income and wealth of married couples were about double that of single males and four times that of single females, and they had about two to three times the pension, retirement, and augmented wealth of single males and females. However, single males in age group 47-64 generally experienced the largest increases in average income, net worth, and retirement wealth of the three groups. Married couples in this age group also saw significant gains in income, wealth, pension wealth, and overall retirement wealth, while single females had only small gains in mean income, wealth, and overall retirement wealth and generally experienced declines in their pension wealth.

Homeowners and renters also followed different financial paths (see Tables 16 and 17 below). In 1998, homeowners had two to three times the income, over seven times the net worth, about three times the pension wealth, twice the retirement wealth, and nearly four times the augmented wealth of renters. Homeowners also had greater gains than renters over the 1983-98 period in terms of income, net worth, pension wealth, and total retirement wealth.

Retirement income rose…

As wealth increased for the average household, so did average expected retirement income among households in the age group 47-64 from 1983 to 1998. Expected retirement income for this group, on the basis of its wealth holdings and its expected pension and Social Security benefits, was a respectable $50,000 (**Table 2**). There were large disparities, though, in the average retirement income different groups could expect: non-Hispanic white households could expect two and half times as much as African American and Hispanic households; married couples 2.4 times as much as single males and 3.3 times as much as single females; and homeowners 3.5 times as much as renters.

Some groups saw substantial gains in their average expected retirement income between 1989 and 1998. For all households in the age group 47-64 the gain was 7%, but the projected gains were somewhat larger for African American and Hispanic households than for white households, greater for single females than for married couples or for single males, and about the same for homeowners and renters. In other words, there seems to have been a slight convergence of expected retirement incomes across different demographic groups, although the disparity between levels of expected retirement income remains large.

TABLE 2. Expected retirement income, age 47-64, 1989 and 1998
(in thousands, 1998 dollars)

	1989	1998	Change 1989-98
1. Expected mean retirement income based on wealth and expected pension and Social Security benefits			
A. All ages 47-64	$46.9	$50.0	7%
1. Age: 47-55	47.2	46.2	-2%
2. Age: 56-64	46.7	55.7	19%
B. All ages 47-64			
1. Non-Hispanic white	54.2	56.0	3%
2. African American or Hispanic	20.4	22.1	8%
3. Married couples	62.1	66.6	7%
4. Single males	26.7	27.8	4%
5. Single females	18.4	20.4	11%
6. Homeowners	55.9	59.7	7%
7. Renters	15.7	17.0	8%
2. Percent of households with expected retirement income less than the poverty line based on wealth holdings and expected pension and Social Security benefits			
A. All ages 47-64	17.2	18.5	1.2
1. Age: 47-55	16.0	19.1	3.1
2. Age: 56-64	18.6	17.5	-1.0
B. All ages 47-64			
1. Non-Hispanic white	8.8	12.8	4.0
2. African American or Hispanic	49.7	43.1	-6.6
3. Married couples	5.5	6.6	1.0
4. Single males	28.7	46.0	17.3
5. Single females	41.3	33.5	-7.8
6. Homeowners	6.3	9.1	2.8
7. Renters	55.5	50.2	-5.3
3. Percent of households with expected retirement income less than 50% of current income based on wealth holdings and expected pension and Social Security benefits			
A. All ages 47-64	29.9	42.5	12.6
1. Age: 47-55	37.0	47.9	10.9
2. Age: 56-64	22.3	34.4	12.0
B. All ages 47-64			
1. Non-Hispanic white	26.1	40.3	14.1
2. African American or Hispanic	43.6	52.7	9.1
3. Married couples	24.2	37.3	13.1
4. Single males	25.5	62.4	36.9
5. Single females	46.1	45.0	-1.1
6. Homeowners	23.5	39.5	15.9
7. Renters	52.1	52.8	0.7

Notes: Households are classified by the age of the head of household.
A 7% real return on assets is assumed for net worth.

Source: Author's computations from the 1983, 1989, and 1998 Survey of Consumer Finances.

...but retirement income adequacy declined

Although there have been substantial gains in retirement income for different groups, retirement income adequacy actually declined from 1989 (the earliest year for which complete data are available) to 1998. For instance, 18.5% of all households in the 47-64 age group in 1998 are expected to be unable to have enough income to cross the poverty line at retirement; this is an increase of 1.2 percentage points compared to 1989. The share of households unable to meet this goal in 1998 is much higher among the black and Hispanic community than among whites; much higher among single males and females than among married couples; and much higher among renters than among homeowners.

Again, considerable progress in meeting the goal of having retirement income above the poverty line was made by black and Hispanic households between 1989 and 1998 (an improvement of 6.6 percentage points), by single females (7.8 percentage points), and by renters (5.3 percentage points). At the same time, the share of households unable to meet this threshold rose among white families, single males, and homeowners.

In terms of replacing current income, 42.5% of households in the 47-64 age group in 1998 will be unable to replace half of their current income at retirement on the basis of their accumulated wealth and their expected pension and Social Security benefits. This represents a sharp deterioration from 1989, when just 29.9% of households would have been unable to meet this goal.

The typical household is worse off in 1998 than in 1989

All in all, the share of middle-age families with expected retirement income shortfalls rose over the 1989-98 period, despite the fact that older Americans became better off *on average* over the 1980s and 1990s. The contraction of traditional defined benefit pension plans and their replacement by defined contribution plans appears to have helped rich older Americans but hurt a large group of lower- and moderate-income households.

Trends in income and wealth

Table 3 illustrates trends in average wealth for the entire American population. Perhaps the most striking result from this table is that median wealth (the wealth of the household in the middle of the distribution) was only 3.8% greater in 1998 than in 1989. After rising by 7.0% between 1983 and 1989, median wealth fell by 17% from 1989 to 1995 and then rose by 24% from 1995 to 1998. One reason for the slow growth in median wealth is evident from the third row of Panel A, which

TABLE 3. Household wealth and income, 1983-98
(in thousands, 1998 dollars)

	1983	1989	1992	1995	1998	Percentage change		
						1983-89	1989-98	1983-98
A. Net worth								
1. Median	$54.6	$58.4	$49.9	$48.8	$60.7	7.0%	3.8%	11.1%
2. Mean	212.6	243.6	236.8	218.8	270.3	14.6%	11.0%	27.1%
3. Percent with zero or negative net worth	15.5	17.9	18.0	18.5	18.0			
B. Financial net worth								
1. Median	11.8	13.9	11.7	10.6	17.8	18.0%	28.0%	51.0%
2. Mean	154.3	181.8	180.5	167.9	212.3	17.8%	16.8%	37.6%
3. Percent with zero or negative financial wealth	25.7	26.8	28.2	28.7	25.7			
Income								
1. Median	33.1	31.6	30.3	32.1	33.4	-4.6%	5.6%	0.8%
2. Mean	46.9	49.0	49.7	46.6	52.3	4.4%	6.7%	11.4%

Notes: The 1983 weights are the full sample 1983 composite weights; and the 1989 weights are the average of the SRC-Design-S1 series (X40131) and the SRC designed based weights (X40125). The 1992 calculations are based on the designed-base weights (X42000), with my adjustments (see Wolff 1996). The 1995 weights are the designed-base Weights (X42000). The 1998 weights are partially designed-based weights (X42001), which account for the systematic deviations from CPS estimates of homeownership by racial/ethnic groups. The 1983, 1989, 1992, and 1995 asset and liability entries are aligned to national balance sheet totals (see Wolff 2001).

Source: Author's computations from the 1983, 1989, 1992, 1995, and 1998 Surveys of Consumer Finances.

shows that the percentage of households with zero or negative net worth increased from 15.5% in 1983 to 18.0% in 1998.

Mean wealth is much higher than median wealth – $270,300 versus $60,700 in 1998. This difference implies that the vast bulk of household wealth is concentrated among the richest families. Mean wealth sharply increased from 1983 to 1989, fell precipitously 1989 to 1995, then, buoyed largely by rising stock prices, surged between 1995 and 1998. Overall, mean wealth was 27.1% higher in 1998 than in 1983 and 11.1% higher than in 1989. The fact that mean wealth increased so much more than median wealth is indicative of rising inequality in the distribution of household wealth over this period.

Median financial wealth was less than $18,000 in 1998, indicating that the average American household had very little savings available for its immediate needs. The time trend for financial wealth is similar to that for household net worth. Median financial wealth rose by 18% between 1983 and 1989, plummeted by 24% from 1989 to 1995, then climbed in 1998, for a net increase of 51%. Between 1983 and 1995, the fraction of households with zero or negative financial wealth rose from 25.7% to 28.7%, then fell back to 25.7% in 1998, a trend that partly explains the trends in median financial wealth.

Mean financial wealth, after increasing by 18% from 1983 to 1989, declined by 8% between 1989 and 1995 and then jumped in 1998, for a net gain of 38%. The bull market appears to be largely responsible for this sharp growth in financial wealth between 1995 and 1998.

Median household income, after falling by 4.6% between 1983 and 1989, grew by 5.6% from 1989 to 1998, for a net change of only about 1%. Mean income rose by 4% from 1983 to 1989, declined by 5% from 1989 to 1995, and then climbed by 11% in 1998, for a net change of about 11%.

In sum, the results point to stagnating living conditions for the average American household, with median net worth growing by only 3.8% and median income by 5.6% between 1989 and 1998.

Wealth trends by age groups

In general, the age-wealth profile apparent in these data tends to follow the life cycle pattern predicted by Modigliani and Brumberg (1954). Mean wealth generally rises with age, peaks at the 65-70 age range, then generally falls with age after that point. Median wealth has a similar pattern, though it tends to peak at earlier ages – typically, in the late 50s or early 60s. The same is true with respect to the percent of households with zero or negative net worth, which tends to peak around age groups 47-58.

Table 4 shows income trends (also see Appendix Tables 1 and 2 for more detail). Among all households in which the head of household is age 47 or over, both mean and median income grew by a respectable 16.2% in real terms (about

**TABLE 4. Household income, age 47 and over, 1983, 1989, and 1998
(in thousands, 1998 dollars)**

	1983	1989	1998	Percentage change 1983-89	1989-98	1983-98
All, age 47 and over						
1. Mean income	$48.2	$49.7	$56.0	3.2%	12.6%	16.2%
2. Median income	27.9	28.4	32.4	1.9%	14.1%	16.3%
Ages 47-64						
1. Mean income	58.2	62.7	70.1	7.6%	11.9%	20.4%
2. Median income	38.6	39.4	44.0	2.3%	11.6%	14.1%
Ages 65 and over						
1. Mean income	33.9	34.4	37.6	1.7%	9.3%	11.2%
2. Median income	17.8	18.9	21.0	6.6%	10.9%	18.3%

Note: Households are classified by the age of the head of household.

Source: Author's computations from the 1983, 1989, and 1998 Survey of Consumer Finances.

1% per year) between 1983 and 1998. The rate of growth was much higher in the 1989-98 period than in the 1983-89 period. For households in the 47-64 age bracket, mean income increased by 20.4%, faster than that among all households age 47 and over, while median income grew by 14.1%, less than that for the entire 47 and over age group. Here, too, gains were greater after 1989 than before. Among elderly households (age 65 and over), mean income rose by only 11.2%, about half the rate for the 47-64 age bracket, while median income climbed 18.3%, much greater than for the younger age group. Once again, gains were greater after 1989 than before.

All five-year age groups showed improvement in mean income over the period from 1983 to 1998 (see Appendix Table 1). Increases were particularly strong for households headed by persons 71 and over and, generally speaking, those in their fifties. Most five-year age groups showed gains in the 1989-98 period, but changes were more mixed in the 1983-89 period. Median income also advanced for all five-year age groups between 1983 and 1998. Gains were again strongest among the 71 and older age groups. Median income rose among most age groups during the 1983-89 and 1989-98 periods. All three-year age groups showed gains in mean income over the 1983-98 period, and all but two showed gains in median income (see Appendix Table 2).

Table 5 shows a similar set of statistics for net worth (also see Appendix Tables 3 and 4). Between 1983 and 1998, mean wealth in real terms increased by a robust 22.0% (or 1.3% per year) among all households ages 47 and over. Median wealth grew even more, 25.5% (or 1.5% per year). Most of the growth in mean

**TABLE 5. Household net worth, age 47 and over, 1983, 1989, and 1998
(in thousands, 1998 dollars)**

| | 1983 | 1989 | 1998 | Percentage change* | | |
				1983-89	1989-98	1983-98
All, age 47 and over						
1. Mean net worth	$343.2	$366.7	$418.6	6.8%	14.2%	22.0%
2. Median net worth	96.8	111.9	121.5	15.6%	8.6%	25.5%
3. Percent of households with zero or negative net worth	7.8%	8.6%	7.5%	0.8	-1.0	-0.3
Ages 47-64						
1. Mean net worth	$343.4	$375.0	$444.6	9.2%	18.6%	29.5%
2. Median net worth	99.7	122.6	110.4	23.0%	-9.9%	10.8%
3. Percent of households with zero or negative net worth	8.4%	9.5%	10.0%	1.2	0.5	1.6
Ages 65 and over						
1. Mean net worth	$343.0	$356.9	$384.9	4.1%	7.8%	12.2%
2. Median net worth	93.8	100.7	133.7	7.3%	32.8%	42.5%
3. Percent of households with zero or negative net worth	7.1%	7.5%	4.4%	0.4	-3.1	-2.7

* Percentage point change for lines showing percent of households with zero or negative net worth.
Note: Households are classified by the age of the head of household.

Source: Author's computations from the 1983, 1989, and 1998 Survey of Consumer Finances.

wealth occurred after 1989, whereas most of the gains in median wealth occurred before 1989. The share of households with zero or negative net worth (an indicator of the wealth position of the bottom of the wealth distribution) rose by 0.8 percentage points between 1983 and 1989, then fell by 1.0 percentage points between 1989 and 1998, for little net change over the entire period.

Among households in the 47-64 age bracket, mean wealth increased by a sizable 29.5% over the 1983-98 period, faster than the growth rate for all households age 47 and over, while median wealth grew by a more modest 10.8%, slower than the rate for all households 47 and over. Here, again, gains in mean wealth were greater after 1989 than before, while the opposite was true for median wealth (in fact, median net worth actually declined from 1989 to 1998). For this age group, the share of households with zero or negative net worth increased in both periods, for a net rise of 1.6 percentage points over the entire 1983-98 period.

Mean wealth grew much more slowly – only 12.2% – among elderly households, while median wealth climbed by a striking 42.5%. Almost all the growth in median net worth occurred after 1989. The proportion of elderly households with no wealth increased slightly between 1983 and 1989, then fell dramatically between 1989 and 1998, by 3.1 percentage points. By 1998, the share of elderly households with no net worth was less than half the share among those age 47-64.

Here again, with only one exception, each five-year age group saw both its mean and median wealth expand over the period from 1983 to 1998 (see Appendix Table 3). Gains were again strongest among the oldest age groups, particularly in terms of median wealth. The percentage of households with zero or negative net worth rose among the younger age groups between 1983 and 1998, but declined among those age 59 and older. Results are similar on the basis of three-year age groups (Appendix Table 4).

Results for financial wealth are shown in **Table 6** (also see Appendix Tables 5 and 6). Median financial wealth climbed by a startling 63.1% (3.3% per year) between 1983 and 1998 among households age 47 and over. Mean financial wealth also grew substantially, by 26.9%. The growth in median financial wealth was

---

TABLE 6. Household financial wealth, age 47 and over, 1983, 1989, and 1998 (in thousands, 1998 dollars)

				Percentage change*		
	1983	1989	1998	1983-89	1989-98	1983-98
All, age 47 and over						
1. Mean financial wealth	$260.6	$279.4	$330.8	7.2%	18.4%	26.9%
2. Median financial wealth	29.8	37.2	48.6	24.8%	30.7%	63.1%
3. Percent of households with zero or negative net worth	16.4%	17.4%	14.4%	1.0	-3.0	-2.0
Ages 47-64						
1. Mean financial wealth	$253.4	$282.6	$362.9	11.5%	28.4%	43.2%
2. Median financial wealth	29.2	37.4	52.6	28.1%	40.5%	80.0%
3. Percent of households with zero or negative net worth	18.4%	18.9%	17.4%	0.5	-1.5	-1.0
Ages 65 and over						
1. Mean financial wealth	$270.7	$275.7	$289.1	1.8%	4.9%	6.8%
2. Median financial wealth	32.0	37.1	45.8	15.8%	23.3%	42.8%
3. Percent of households with zero or negative net worth	13.4%	15.6%	10.5%	2.1	-5.1	-2.9

* Percentage point change for lines showing percent of households with zero or negative financial wealth.
Note: Households are classified by the age of the head of household.

Source: Author's computations from the 1983, 1989, and 1998 Survey of Consumer Finances.

about evenly split between the 1983-89 and 1989-98 periods, while most of the growth in mean financial wealth occurred after 1989. The percent of households with zero or negative financial wealth increased by 1.0 percentage points between 1983 and 1989, then declined by 3.0 percentage points over the 1983-98 period, for a net decline of 2.0 percentage points.

Among households in 47-64 age group, median financial wealth surged by 80.0% (or 3.9% per year) between 1983 and 1998, while mean financial wealth climbed by a more moderate though still respectable 43.2%. Both mean and median financial wealth increased more for this age group than among all households aged 47 and over. The share of households with no financial wealth increased by 0.5 percentage points from 1983 to 1989, then fell by 1.5 percentage points from 1989 to 1998, for a net change of -1.0 percentage points.

Among elderly households, median financial wealth climbed by 42.8% between 1983 and 1998, while mean financial wealth inched up by only 6.8%. The share of households with no financial wealth, after rising by 2.1 percentage points from 1983 to 1989, fell by a huge 5.1 percentage points from 1989 to 1998, for a net decline of 2.9 percentage points. By 1998, the share of households with no financial wealth was much lower among the elderly than among those in age bracket 47-64.

Almost all five-year age groups age 47 and over saw increases in their mean and median financial wealth over the period 1983-98 and reductions in the share with zero or negative financial wealth (see Appendix Table 5). Those over age 70 did particularly well. Results are similar based on three-year age groups (see Appendix Table 6).

Wealth and homeownership

Among all American households, the homeownership rate (the percent of households owning their own home) declined slightly between 1983 and 1989, from 63.4% to 62.8%, then markedly improved to 66.3% in 1998, for a net gain of 2.8 percentage points over the entire 15 years (see Appendix Table 8). Among all households, mean home equity (defined as the market value of the primary residence less any outstanding mortgage debt on the property) rose by 5.8% between 1983 and 1989 and then fell by 6.0% from 1989 to 1998, for no net gain. Median home equity actually declined in both periods and by 21.9% over the full 15 years.

The story is somewhat different among older households (**Table 7**). Among all households age 47 and over, mean home equity grew by 5.6% between 1983 and 1989, then remained almost unchanged from 1989 to 1998, for a net gain of 6.3%. In contrast, median home equity, after declining by 8.2% from 1983 to 1989, leapt by 12.2% from 1989 to 1998, for a net change of 3.0%. The homeownership rate for this group remained unchanged between 1983 and 1989, then increased by 1.1 percentage points from 1989 to 1998.

**TABLE 7. Household homeownership, age 47 and over, 1983, 1989, and 1998
(in thousands, 1998 dollars)**

	1983	1989	1998	Percentage change* 1983-89	1989-98	1983-98
All, age 47 and over						
1. Mean home equity	$82.7	$87.3	$87.8	5.6%	0.7%	6.3%
2. Median home equity	57.3	52.6	59.0	-8.2%	12.2%	3.0%
3. Homeownership rate	75.9%	75.8%	76.9%	0.0	1.1	1.0
Ages 47-64						
1. Mean home equity	$90.0	$92.4	$81.7	2.7%	-11.6%	-9.2%
2. Median home equity	64.5	57.8	50.6	-10.3%	-12.5%	-21.5%
3. Homeownership rate	77.0%	77.3%	75.3%	0.3	-2.0	-1.7
Ages 65 and over						
1. Mean home equity	$72.3	$81.3	$95.8	12.4%	17.9%	32.5%
2. Median home equity	49.1	50.0	67.0	1.7%	34.1%	36.5%
3. Homeownership rate	74.3%	74.1%	79.0%	-0.2	4.9	4.7

* Percentage point change for lines showing home ownership rate.
Note: Households are classified by the age of the head of household.

Source: Author's computations from the 1983, 1989, and 1998 Survey of Consumer Finances.

Among age group 47 to 64, both mean and median home equity fell in real terms between 1983 and 1998; the latter dropped by 21.5%. All of the decline in mean home equity occurred after 1989, while the fall at the median was about equally split before and after 1989. The decline in home equity reflected mainly the rise in mortgage debt, rather the decline in house values. This group also saw its homeownership rate fall by 1.7 percentage points over the 1983-98 period, with all of the decline happening after 1989. In contrast, both mean and median home equity surged among elderly households – by 32.5 and 36.5%, respectively – with most of the gains occurring after 1989. In addition, the homeownership rate, after falling by 0.2 percentage points from 1983 to 1989, climbed by 4.9 percentage points from 1989 to 1998, for a net gain of 4.7 percentage points.

Between 1983 and 1998, both mean and median home equity generally declined among five-year age groups under the age of 65 but increased among those age 65 and over (see Appendix Table 7). Increases were especially high among households over age 70. Among the non-elderly households, the declines in mean and median home equity were more pronounced during the years 1989 to 1998. Homeownership rates generally fell during the 1980s among households age 47-70 and fell during the 1990s among households age 47-58. Over the entire period, results were mixed for these age groups. However, homeownership rates rose in both periods for households over age 70 and improved considerably over the entire 15-year period. Results are similar based on three-year age groups (Appendix Table 8).

Retirement wealth

Between 1983 and 1998, average holdings of defined contribution (DC) pension accounts and the percentage of households holding these kinds of plans rose precipitously (see **Table 8** and Appendix Tables 9 and 11). Among all households (Appendix Table 11), the average value of these accounts increased tenfold between 1983 and 1998, from $3,600 (in 1998 dollars) to $36,800. Among households age 47 and over (Appendix Table 9), the average value also increased about tenfold over the period, from $5,000 (in 1998 dollars) to $53,100. Among age group 47-64, the increase was by a factor of about 8.4, while among elderly households the increase was by a factor of 18.3 (Table 8). Most of the growth occurred after 1989. Moreover, the share of households age 47 and over holding a defined contribution pension account surged from 7.8% in 1983 to 47.8% in 1998, or by almost 40 percentage points. The proportion holding pension accounts advanced by 48 percentage points among households in age group 47-64 and by 30 percentage points among elderly households. In 1998, about 60% of households in the 47-64 age range held some form of defined contribution account, compared to 32% of elderly households.

As shown in Appendix Table 9, mean defined contribution pension wealth rose strongly with age in 1998, from $51,800 among age group 47-52 to $104,800 for age group 59-64, and then tailed off with age, down to $8,200 among those age 77 and over. After age 64, the ownership rate of these accounts generally fell with age, reaching a low of 14.0% for households age 77 and over. Large increases in both the ownership rate and mean holdings of defined contribution pension accounts were experienced by all five-year age groups between 1983 and 1998 – particularly after 1989.

Opposite trends are apparent for defined benefit (DB) pension wealth. Among all households (Appendix Table 11), the average value of defined benefit pension wealth fell by 30% between 1983 and 1998, from $50,900 (in 1998 dollars) to $35.600. The share of all households with defined benefit pension wealth also fell, by 17.3 percentage points, from 52.6% to 35.3%. Among households in age group 47 and over (Appendix Table 9), mean pension wealth fell by 15% over this period, and the share with defined benefit pensions fell by 21.9 percentage points (from 67.8 to 45.9%). Most of the loss in coverage occurred during the 1989-98 period. Losses were particularly marked for age group 47-64, who saw their mean defined benefit pension wealth decline by 39% between 1983 and 1998 and the share covered by defined benefit plans fall by 26.5 percentage points (Table 8). However, the average value of defined benefit plans actually rose by 36% among elderly house-

TABLE 8. Household retirement wealth, age 47 and over, 1983, 1989, and 1998
(in thousands, 1998 dollars)

	1998 mean value	Percentage change			Percent holding asset, 1998	Percentage point change		
		1983-89	1989-98	1983-98		1983-89	1989-98	1983-98
All, age 47 and over								
1. Mean DC pension wealth	$53.1	90%	458%	959%	47.8%	8.1	31.9	39.9
2. Mean DB pension wealth	62.8	-2%	-14%	-15%	45.9	-8.9	-13.0	-21.9
3. Mean DC + DB pension wealth	115.9	4%	41%	47%	69.5	-3.8	4.4	0.6
4. Mean Social Security wealth	123.1	-18%	8%	-11%	97.7	12.7	-1.1	11.6
5. Mean DC + DB pension wealth + Social Security wealth	239.1	-10%	22%	10%	98.3	2.2	-1.1	1.1
6. Median DC + DB pension wealth + Social Security wealth	171.6	-22%	20%	-7%				
Ages 47-64								
1. Mean DC pension wealth	69.2	118%	330%	838%	59.7	16.4	31.4	47.8
2. Mean DB pension wealth	52.7	-18%	-26%	-39%	42.4	-8.0	-18.6	-26.5

3. Mean DC + DB pension wealth	121.9	-8%	40%	29%	73.7	1.9	1.6	3.5
4. Mean Social Security wealth	121.7	-24%	15%	-13%	99.0	6.4	0.5	6.9
5. Mean DC + DB pension wealth + Social Security wealth	243.5	-18%	26%	4%	99.4	2.3	0.0	2.3
6. Median DC + DB pension wealth + Social Security wealth	175.2	-29%	25%	-11%				
Ages 65 and over								
1. Mean DC pension wealth	32.3	7%	1706%	1826%	32.3	-0.8	31.0	30.2
2. Mean DB pension wealth	75.9	35%	1%	36%	50.4	-9.7	-6.1	-15.8
3. Mean DC + DB pension wealth	108.3	34%	40%	89%	64.0	-10.3	7.3	-3.0
4. Mean Social Security wealth	125.0	-9%	2%	-8%	96.0	21.6	-3.1	18.5
5. Mean DC + DB pension wealth + Social Security wealth	233.3	4%	17%	21%	96.8	2.0	-2.6	-0.5
6. Median DC + DB pension wealth + Social Security wealth	169.8	-8%	12%	4%				

Note: Households are classified by the age of the head of household.

Source: Author's computations from the 1983, 1989, and 1998 Survey of Consumer Finances.

hold over this period, though the share covered fell by 15.8 percentage points. As with defined contribution pensions, the average amount of defined benefit pension wealth generally rises with age until age group 65-70 and then declines after that. The same pattern is observable with the share of households covered by defined benefit pension plans.

Has the spread of defined contribution pension plans adequately compensated for the decline in traditional defined benefit pension coverage? The results in line 3 of Table 8, which show the sum of defined contribution and defined benefit pension wealth, indicate that the answer is "yes." Total pension wealth increased for all age groups between 1983 and 1998. For all households age 47 and over, the mean value of total pension wealth climbed by 47%. Among those in age group 47-64, the mean value increased by 29%, with all the growth occurring after 1989; among elderly households, the mean value jumped by 89%, with the gains about evenly split before and after 1989. As shown in Appendix Table 9, percentage increases in the mean value of total pensions were much lower for households between ages 47 and 58, averaging around 14%. However, households in the age group 59 to 76 saw their average total pension wealth almost double. Even households in age group 77 and over enjoyed a 59% increase in their average total pension holdings.

The percentage of households covered by either a defined contribution or a defined benefit plan also rose over the 1983-98 period, though at a more modest pace. The share of all households covered by one plan or the other grew by a full 10.2 percentage points over the period, from 54.4 to 64.6% (Appendix Table 11). Among households in age group 47 and over (Appendix Table 9), the share increased slightly (from 68.9% to 69.5%). Among the 47-64 age group (Table 8), the proportion rose by 3.5 percentage points, to 73.7% in 1998, while among the elderly, the share fell by 3.0 percentage points, down to 64.0% in 1998. The share of households age 47-76 covered by pensions grew by two percentage points or more for each age group (Appendix Table 9); households in age group 77 and over were the only ones to see their coverage slip, by 11.0 percentage points, with all the decline occurring between 1983 and 1989.

In contrast, as shown in Table 8, Social Security wealth generally declined among older Americans. The average value of Social Security wealth among households age 47 and over fell by 11% between 1983 and 1998, from $138,500 to $123,100 (Appendix Table 10). Among all households, the decline was 16% (see panel G of Appendix Table 11). Households in the 47-64 age bracket saw their average Social Security wealth decline by 13% between 1983 and 1998, while elderly households experienced an 8% decline (Table 8). In all cases, Social Security wealth first fell during the years 1983 to 1989, then rose from 1989 to 1998. Decreases in average Social Security wealth occurred for all age groups and were particularly marked for age groups 53-58 and 59-64 (Appendix Table 10). Almost all five-year age groups saw their average Social Security wealth fall from 1983 to 1989, and almost all experienced gains from 1989 to 1998. However, the losses sustained in the earlier period were greater than the increases in the latter period.

In contrast, Social Security coverage also expanded over the period from 1983 to 1998. Among all households, the share with Social Security wealth increased by 16.0 percentage points, from 82.4% to 98.4% (see panel H of Appendix Table 11). Among households in age group 47 and over, the share grew by 11.6 percentage points, with all the gain occurring before 1989 (Table 8). The share increased by 6.9 percentage points among households in age group 47-64 and by 18.5 percentage points among elderly households. Here, too, almost all the gains occurred before 1989. The share of households covered by Social Security increased among all five-year age groups, particularly over the 1983-89 period (Appendix Table 10). Gains were especially high among the 65 and older age groups.

Turning to total retirement wealth, i.e., the sum of defined contribution pensions, defined benefit pension wealth, and Social Security wealth, growth was flat for all households combined between 1983 and 1998 (panel I of Appendix Table 11) because gains in total pension wealth were offset by losses in Social Security wealth. However, among households in age group 47 and over (Table 8), mean retirement wealth grew by 10% over this period; it fell 10% between 1983 and 1989, then rose 22% from 1989 to 1998. The proportion of households with some form of retirement wealth also rose slightly, from 97.2% to 98.3% (Appendix Table 10). In contrast, median retirement wealth generally fell over the 1983 to 1998 period (Appendix Table 11). Among all households, it declined by 21%, from $146,300 to $115,000. Among households in age group 47 and over (Appendix Table 10), median retirement wealth decreased by 7%, from $184,200 to $171,600. There was a steep decline in median retirement wealth between 1983 and 1989, followed by a sizeable recovery between 1989 and 1998, though the net change was still negative.

The pattern is similar for the 47-64 age group (Table 8). Between 1983 and 1998, mean retirement wealth increased by 4%, median retirement wealth fell by 11%, and the share of households with retirement wealth increased by 2.3 percentage points, to 99.4%. In contrast, mean retirement wealth among the elderly rose by 21% over the 1983-98 period, median retirement wealth grew by 4%, and the share of elderly households with retirement wealth fell by 0.5 percentage points, to 96.8%. As shown in Appendix Table 10, mean retirement wealth among households in age groups 47-52 and 53-58 changed little over that period. However, mean retirement wealth increased by between 24% and 32% among households in the 59-76 age range and by 14% among the oldest age group. As noted above, the share of households in age group 47 and over covered by either a pension plan or Social Security increased slightly over the period, from 97.2% in 1983 to 98.3% in 1998. Changes were relatively small for individual age groups as well. The biggest drops in median retirement wealth occurred among age groups 53-58 and 59-64 (by about 10%). Median retirement wealth grew by between 9% and 18% among the 65-plus age groups.

Table 9 provides a breakdown of mean retirement wealth by wealth class, defined in terms of net worth. Net worth and retirement wealth seem to be strongly correlated. Among all households age 47 and over, mean retirement wealth ranged from a low of $105,200 for the lowest wealth class to $581,300 for the top wealth class in 1998 – almost a six-fold difference. Even more striking is the fact that mean retirement wealth declined among the five lowest wealth classes (up to a net worth of $500,000) and increased only in the top two wealth classes. Indeed, it surged by 43.8% for the top wealth class ($1,000,000 or more in net worth).

TABLE 9. Mean retirement wealth by wealth class, age 47 and over, 1983, 1989, and 1998
(in thousands, 1998 dollars)

	1983	1989	1998	Percentage change 1983-89	1989-98.	1983-98
All, age 47 and over						
Under $25,000	$126.2	$94.0	$105.2	-25.5%	11.9%	-16.7%
$25-000-$49,999	175.2	146.6	146.2	-16.4%	-0.2%	-16.6%
$50,000-$99,999	198.8	162.4	147.4	-18.3%	-9.3%	-25.9%
$100-000-$249,999	242.1	191.7	182.0	-20.8%	-5.1%	-24.8%
$250,000-$499,999	274.0	234.4	253.1	-14.4%	8.0%	-7.6%
$500,000-$999,999	302.1	316.6	304.6	4.8%	-3.8%	0.8%
$1,000,000 or over	404.3	392.1	581.3	-3.0%	48.3%	43.8%
Ages 47-64						
Under $25,000	131.8	79.9	107.5	-39.4%	34.6%	-18.4%
$25-000-$49,999	182.4	125.2	136.0	-31.4%	8.7%	-25.4%
$50,000-$99,999	206.3	155.1	166.0	-24.8%	7.0%	-19.6%
$100-000-$249,999	263.0	198.4	177.0	-24.6%	-10.8%	-32.7%
$250,000-$499,999	297.5	238.5	260.2	-19.8%	9.1%	-12.6%
$500,000-$999,999	335.7	306.3	298.0	-8.7%	-2.7%	-11.2%
$1,000,000 or over	431.1	367.8	608.1	-14.7%	65.3%	41.1%
Ages 65 and over						
Under $25,000	119.3	109.6	101.5	-8.2%	-7.4%	-15.0%
$25-000-$49,999	166.0	168.5	163.5	1.5%	-3.0%	-1.5%
$50,000-$99,999	187.2	169.3	120.6	-9.6%	-28.8%	-35.6%
$100-000-$249,999	208.9	182.6	187.2	-12.6%	2.5%	-10.4%
$250,000-$499,999	240.1	229.6	245.4	-4.4%	6.9%	2.2%
$500,000-$999,999	257.3	329.1	313.5	27.9%	-4.7%	21.9%
$1,000,000 or over	362.0	426.7	542.2	17.9%	27.1%	49.8%

Notes: Households are classified by net worth (HDW) in 1998 dollars.
Key: Retirement wealth (RW) = DC pension accounts + DB pension wealth + Social Security wealth.

Source: Author's computations from the 1983, 1989, and 1998 Survey of Consumer Finances.

Demographic breakdowns

The next eight tables illustrate breakdowns of both income and wealth by age and demographic characteristics. In terms of race and ethnicity (**Tables 10** and **11** and Appendix Table 12), there are marked differences in retirement wealth between non-Hispanic whites on the one hand and African Americans and Hispanics on the other.[1] In 1998, for example, the mean pension wealth (defined contribution plus defined benefit holdings) of the latter group averaged about half that of non-Hispanic white households, while mean Social Security wealth averaged about 60% (Table 10). All told, mean (total) retirement wealth among blacks and Hispanics was a little more than half that of non-Hispanic whites. The disparities tended to widen with age (Appendix Table 12).

Between 1983 and 1998, mean pension wealth grew much more among non-Hispanic white households than among black and Hispanic households – 49.1% versus 4.1% among households in age 47 and over. Among households in age groups 47-64, mean pension wealth increased by 33.1% among whites but *declined* by 17.9% among blacks and Hispanics. However, among elderly households, average pension wealth surged by almost the same amount for the two groups – 87.1% and 89.3%, respectively. Social Security wealth declined for both groups but much more for African Americans and Hispanics than for non-Hispanic whites – 9.3% versus 24.4% among age group 47 and over. Altogether, mean retirement wealth increased by 6.1% among white households in the 47-64 age group, compared to a 19.9% decline among black and Hispanic households. Among elderly households, mean retirement wealth surged by 23.0% for white households but declined by 2.7% for black and Hispanic households.

There are also marked differences in income and wealth between non-Hispanic whites on the one hand and African Americans and Hispanics on the other (Table 11). In 1998, for example, the mean income of the latter group averaged about half that of non-Hispanic white households, while mean wealth holdings averaged about a quarter. The wealth disparity tended to widen with age (see Appendix Table 12).

Despite these large disparities, both income and wealth tended to advance more among black and Hispanic households than among non-Hispanic white households over the 1983-98 period. Among those households in age group 47 and over (Table 11), mean income grew by 15.1% and mean net worth by 20.6% among whites, compared to 20.6% and 66.7%, respectively, among blacks and Hispanics. Among households in the 47-64 age bracket, mean income actually rose more among whites than among blacks and Hispanics, while mean wealth grew much more among the latter. Among elderly households, both mean income and mean wealth grew three to four times as much among blacks and Hispanics than among whites. However, all told, mean augmented wealth still advanced somewhat more among whites households (9.1% for those age 47 and over) than among black and Hispanic households (4.4%). Similar disparities exist for the two age sub-groups.

**TABLE 10. Retirement wealth by race/ethnicity, age 47 and over,
1983, 1989, and 1998
(in thousands, 1998 dollars)**

Category	Mean value			Percentage change		
	1983	1989	1998	1983-89	1989-98	1983-98
A. Non-Hispanic white						
All, Age 47 and over						
Mean DC + DB pension wealth	$84.4	$89.9	$125.9	6.4%	40.1%	49.1%
Mean Social Security wealth	144.9	125.4	131.4	-13.5%	4.8%	-9.3%
Mean retirement wealth	229.3	215.2	257.3	-6.1%	19.5%	12.2%
Ages 47-64						
Mean DC + DB pension wealth	101.3	100.9	134.8	-0.4%	33.6%	33.1%
Mean Social Security wealth	148.3	118.8	130.1	-19.9%	9.6%	-12.3%
Mean retirement wealth	249.6	219.6	264.9	-12.0%	20.6%	6.1%
Ages 65 and over						
Mean DC + DB pension wealth	61.8	78.0	115.7	26.1%	48.4%	87.1%
Mean Social Security wealth	140.2	132.5	132.8	-5.5%	0.2%	-5.3%
Mean retirement wealth	202.1	210.5	248.5	4.2%	18.1%	23.0%
B. African American or Hispanic						
All, age 47 and over						
Mean DC + DB pension wealth	54.3	45.1	56.5	-17.0%	25.5%	4.1%
Mean Social Security wealth	103.1	66.6	77.9	-35.4%	16.9%	-24.4%
Mean retirement wealth	157.4	111.7	134.5	-29.0%	20.4%	-14.6%
Ages 47-64						
Mean DC + DB pension wealth	66.7	43.7	54.8	-34.5%	25.3%	-17.9%
Mean Social Security wealth	103.5	61.1	81.6	-41.0%	33.6%	-21.2%
Mean retirement wealth	170.2	104.8	136.4	-38.4%	30.1%	-19.9%
Ages 65 and over						
Mean DC + DB pension wealth	31.8	47.2	60.2	48.4%	27.6%	9.3%
Mean Social Security wealth	102.4	75.4	70.4	-26.3%	-6.7%	-31.2%
Mean retirement wealth	134.2	122.6	130.6	-8.6%	6.5%	-2.7%

Notes: Households are classified by the age of the head of household. Asians and other races are excluded from the table because of small sample sizes.
Key: Retirement wealth (RW) = DC pension accounts + DB pension wealth + Social Security wealth.

Source: Author's computations from the 1983, 1989, and 1998 Survey of Consumer Finances.

Among age group 59 to 64, increases in mean income and mean net worth were comparable for the two racial groups (see Appendix Table 12). However, while pension wealth, total retirement wealth, and augmented wealth advanced strongly among non-Hispanic whites, they all declined for black and Hispanic families. Among age group 65 to 70, growth in mean income and net worth was small among non-Hispanic white households, while black and Hispanic households experienced robust gains. Gains in defined benefit pension wealth among black and

TABLE 11. Income and wealth by race/ethnicity, age 47 and over, 1983, 1989, and 1998
(in thousands, 1998 dollars)

Category	Mean value			Percentage change		
	1983	1989	1998	1983-89	1989-98	1983-98
A. Non-Hispanic white						
All, age 47 and over						
Mean income	$52.3	$56.0	$60.2	7.0%	7.6%	15.1%
Mean net worth (HDW)	392.8	435.9	473.7	11.0%	8.7%	20.6%
Mean augmented wealth	616.6	640.1	672.6	3.8%	5.1%	9.1%
Ages 47-64						
Mean income	63.8	71.9	77.5	12.7%	7.7%	21.4%
Mean net worth (HDW)	398.6	447.1	514.6	12.2%	15.1%	29.1%
Mean augmented wealth	639.8	647.4	702.1	1.2%	8.4%	9.7%
Ages 65 and over						
Mean income	36.8	38.7	40.2	5.1%	3.8%	9.1%
Mean net worth (HDW)	385.1	423.7	426.4	10.0%	0.6%	10.7%
Mean augmented wealth	585.4	632.1	638.4	8.0%	1.0%	9.1%
B. African American or Hispanic						
All, age 47 and over						
Mean income	25.7	22.7	31.0	-11.7%	36.6%	20.6%
Mean net worth (HDW)	70.3	74.6	117.2	6.1%	57.2%	66.7%
Mean augmented wealth	225.3	183.5	235.2	-18.5%	28.2%	4.4%
Ages 47-64						
Mean income	31.6	28.1	35.9	-11.0%	27.4%	13.4%
Mean net worth (HDW)	68.5	92.6	128.4	35.1%	38.8%	87.4%
Mean augmented wealth	235.7	192.8	242.0	-18.2%	25.5%	2.6%
Ages 65 and over						
Mean income	14.8	14.1	20.9	-5.1%	48.0%	40.5%
Mean net worth (HDW)	73.5	46.3	94.0	-37.1%	103.1%	27.8%
Mean augmented wealth	206.3	168.9	221.3	-18.2%	31.0%	7.2%

Notes: Households are classified by the age of the head of household. Asians and other races are excluded from the table because of small sample sizes.
Key: Augmented wealth = net worth less PCSV (HDWX) + retirement wealth (RW).

Source: Author's computations from the 1983, 1989, and 1998 Survey of Consumer Finances.

Hispanic households also outpaced those among whites in the 65-70 age group, though Social Security wealth fell among the former but remained unchanged among the latter. As a result, mean retirement wealth advanced more among white households than among black and Hispanic households, but gains in augmented wealth were larger among blacks and Hispanics. Among the oldest age group, gains in net worth were greater among black and Hispanic households than among non-Hispanic white households, though the reverse was the case for income and both pension and Social Security wealth. As a result, augmented wealth showed robust advances for whites but declined slightly among black and Hispanic households.

Tables 12 and **13** (and Appendix Table 13) show breakdowns by both the age and the education level of the head of household. Among those with less than 12 years of schooling, total pension wealth was about 15% that of the college educated (Table 12). On the other hand, the mean Social Security wealth of households with less than 12 years of schooling was about 60% that of households in the

TABLE 12. Retirement wealth by education, age 47 and over, 1983, 1989, and 1998 (in thousands, 1998 dollars)

Category	Mean value			Percentage change		
	1983	1989	1998	1983-89	1989-98	1983-98
A. Less than 12 years of schooling						
All, age 47 and over						
Mean DC + DB pension wealth	$42.5	$47.2	$36.0	11.1%	-23.8%	-15.4%
Mean Social Security wealth	120.0	92.6	84.2	-22.8%	-9.0%	-29.8%
Mean retirement wealth	162.5	139.8	120.2	-14.0%	-14.0%	-26.0%
Ages 47-64						
Mean DC + DB pension wealth	46.7	52.3	34.1	12.0%	-34.8%	-27.0%
Mean Social Security wealth	126.2	78.0	71.3	-38.2%	-8.6%	-43.5%
Mean retirement wealth	172.9	130.3	105.4	-24.7%	-19.1%	-39.1%
Ages 65 and over						
Mean DC + DB pension wealth	38.7	42.6	37.2	10.2%	-12.7%	-3.8%
Mean Social Security wealth	114.3	104.5	93.1	-8.6%	-10.9%	-18.5%
Mean retirement wealth	152.9	147.1	130.3	-3.8%	-11.4%	-14.8%
B. 12 years of schooling						
All, age 47 and over						
Mean DC + DB pension wealth	76.5	88.0	73.0	15.0%	-17.0%	-4.6%
Mean Social Security wealth	148.4	138.1	130.5	-7.0%	-5.5%	-12.0%
Mean retirement wealth	224.9	226.1	203.5	0.5%	-10.0%	-9.5%
Ages 47-64						
Mean DC + DB pension wealth	84.4	78.8	71.3	-6.6%	-9.5%	-15.5%
Mean Social Security wealth	143.1	124.7	133.7	-12.8%	7.2%	-6.6%
Mean retirement wealth	227.5	203.5	205.0	-10.5%	0.7%	-9.9%
Ages 65 and over						
Mean DC + DB pension wealth	61.3	106.3	75.1	73.4%	-29.4%	22.4%
Mean Social Security wealth	158.6	164.6	126.8	3.8%	-23.0%	-20.1%
Mean retirement wealth	219.9	270.9	201.8	23.2%	-25.5%	-8.2%

continues

same age groups headed by college graduates. The mean retirement wealth of the former was about a third that of the latter, and mean augmented wealth (Table 13) averaged about 15% to 20% that of college graduates. Holdings of total pension wealth among high school graduates (Table 12) ranged from a quarter to a third those of college graduates, and total retirement wealth about half. The pension holdings of those with between 13 and 15 years of schooling ran about 40% that of college graduates, and their retirement wealth about 60%.

TABLE 12 (continued). Retirement wealth by education, age 47 and over, 1983, 1989, and 1998
(in thousands, 1998 dollars)

Category	Mean value			Percentage change		
	1983	1989	1998	1983-89	1989-98	1983-98
C. 13-15 years of schooling						
All, age 47 and over						
Mean DC + DB pension wealth	$96.1	$111.0	$96.4	15.5%	-13.1%	0.3%
Mean Social Security wealth	140.5	128.1	131.7	-8.8%	2.9%	-6.2%
Mean retirement wealth	236.6	239.0	228.1	1.0%	-4.6%	-3.6%
Ages 47-64						
Mean DC + DB pension wealth	114.3	93.4	89.9	-18.2%	-3.8%	-21.4%
Mean Social Security wealth	136.4	117.1	134.5	-14.1%	14.9%	-1.3%
Mean retirement wealth	250.6	210.5	224.4	-16.0%	6.6%	-10.5%
Ages 65 and over						
Mean DC + DB pension wealth	63.1	158.7	108.0	151.4%	-31.9%	71.2%
Mean Social Security wealth	148.0	157.9	126.7	6.7%	-19.7%	-14.4%
Mean retirement wealth	211.1	316.6	234.8	50.0%	-25.8%	11.2%
D. 16 or more years of schooling						
All, age 47 and over						
Mean DC + DB pension wealth	163.6	202.6	244.2	23.8%	20.5%	49.3%
Mean Social Security wealth	169.9	163.3	142.3	-3.9%	-12.8%	-16.2%
Mean retirement wealth	333.5	365.9	386.5	9.7%	5.6%	15.9%
Ages 47-64						
Mean DC + DB pension wealth	175.6	188.2	233.2	7.2%	23.9%	32.8%
Mean Social Security wealth	164.5	155.1	128.6	-5.7%	-17.1%	-21.9%
Mean retirement wealth	340.2	343.4	361.8	0.9%	5.4%	6.4%
Ages 65 and over						
Mean DC + DB pension wealth	133.2	230.7	266.3	73.2%	15.4%	99.9%
Mean Social Security wealth	183.6	179.3	170.1	-2.4%	-5.1%	-7.4%
Mean retirement wealth	316.8	409.9	436.3	29.4%	6.4%	37.7%

Note: Households are classified by the age and education of the head of household.
Key: Retirement wealth (RW) = DC pension accounts + DB pension wealth + Social Security wealth.

Source: Author's computations from the 1983, 1989, and 1998 Survey of Consumer Finances.

The pattern was mixed in terms of growth over the 1983-98 period. Among households headed by someone with less than 12 years of schooling, mean pension wealth fell among age groups 47 and over, 47-64, and 65 and over. Social Security wealth declined for all age groups, as did average retirement wealth. Among high school graduates, average pension wealth fell by 15.5% among age group 47-64 but rose by 22.4% among the elderly. Social Security wealth decreased among all age groups, as did retirement wealth. Among those with one to three years of college,

TABLE 13. Income and wealth by education, age 47 and over, 1983, 1989, and 1998
(in thousands, 1998 dollars)

Category	Mean value			Percentage change		
	1983	1989	1998	1983-89	1989-98	1983-98
A. Less than 12 years of schooling						
All, age 47 and over						
Mean income	$23.1	$24.6	$22.0	6.1%	-10.3%	-4.8%
Mean net worth (HDW)	108.2	148.4	106.1	37.2%	-28.5%	-1.9%
Mean augmented wealth	270.0	285.8	219.1	5.8%	-23.3%	-18.8%
Ages 47-64						
Mean income	29.6	30.3	26.1	2.4%	-14.0%	-11.9%
Mean net worth (HDW)	106.7	136.7	94.1	28.2%	-31.2%	-11.8%
Mean augmented wealth	278.7	262.1	187.6	-6.0%	-28.4%	-32.7%
Ages 65 and over						
Mean income	17.2	19.9	19.3	15.3%	-3.1%	11.8%
Mean net worth (HDW)	109.6	157.9	114.3	44.1%	-27.6%	4.4%
Mean augmented wealth	262.0	305.0	240.7	16.4%	-21.1%	-8.1%
B. 12 years of schooling						
All, age 47 and over						
Mean income	40.7	47.2	36.8	15.9%	-22.0%	-9.6%
Mean net worth (HDW)	244.1	348.5	238.7	42.8%	-31.5%	-2.2%
Mean augmented wealth	466.7	567.4	418.0	21.6%	-26.3%	-10.4%
Ages 47-64						
Mean income	44.9	53.7	41.4	19.4%	-22.8%	-7.8%
Mean net worth (HDW)	224.3	323.8	198.5	44.4%	-38.7%	-11.5%
Mean augmented wealth	448.2	516.6	374.7	15.3%	-27.5%	-16.4%
Ages 65 and over						
Mean income	32.4	34.2	31.4	5.4%	-8.3%	-3.3%
Mean net worth (HDW)	282.5	397.7	286.1	40.8%	-28.1%	1.3%
Mean augmented wealth	502.4	668.6	468.9	33.1%	-29.9%	-6.7%

continues

pension wealth rose strongly among the elderly (71.2%) but declined by 21.4% among age group 47-64. Social Security wealth fell slightly for age group 47-64 and by 14.4% among the elderly. Total retirement wealth fell by 10.5% in age group 47-64 but rose by 11.2% among elderly households. Among college graduates, average pension wealth rose strongly among all groups, Social Security wealth fell, and retirement wealth rose, particularly among the elderly (37.7%).

Among those with less than 12 years of schooling, mean income, net worth,

TABLE 13 (continued). Income and wealth by education, age 47 and over, 1983, 1989, and 1998
(in thousands, 1998 dollars)

Category	Mean value			Percentage change		
	1983	1989	1998	1983-89	1989-98	1983-98
C. 13-15 years of schooling						
All, age 47 and over						
Mean income	$56.7	$68.4	$52.0	20.7%	-24.0%	-8.2%
Mean net worth (HDW)	455.9	565.8	361.1	24.1%	-36.2%	-20.8%
Mean augmented wealth	683.6	791.6	549.3	15.8%	-30.6%	-19.6%
Ages 47-64						
Mean income	63.9	69.9	60.3	9.3%	-13.8%	-5.8%
Mean net worth (HDW)	423.3	380.4	322.7	-10.1%	-15.2%	-23.8%
Mean augmented wealth	664.9	575.7	502.2	-13.4%	-12.8%	-24.5%
Ages 65 and over						
Mean income	43.5	64.4	37.4	48.1%	-42.0%	-14.1%
Mean net worth (HDW)	514.9	1069.8	429.5	107.8%	-59.8%	-16.6%
Mean augmented wealth	717.6	1378.6	633.1	92.1%	-54.1%	-11.8%
D. 16 or more years of schooling						
All, age 47 and over						
Mean income	116.8	144.2	108.2	23.4%	-24.9%	-7.3%
Mean net worth (HDW)	1004.8	1159.8	918.9	15.4%	-20.8%	-8.6%
Mean augmented wealth	1321.2	1486.8	1172.8	12.5%	-21.1%	-11.2%
Ages 47-64						
Mean income	121.2	157.8	124.6	30.3%	-21.1%	2.8%
Mean net worth (HDW)	853.4	1090.2	923.3	27.8%	-15.3%	8.2%
Mean augmented wealth	1171.1	1379.9	1134.6	17.8%	-17.8%	-3.1%
Ages 65 and over						
Mean income	105.7	117.4	75.3	11.1%	-35.8%	-28.7%
Mean net worth (HDW)	1389.4	1295.9	909.9	-6.7%	-29.8%	-34.5%
Mean augmented wealth	1702.4	1695.9	1249.9	-0.4%	-26.3%	-26.6%

Note: Households are classified by the age and education of the head of household.
Key: Augmented wealth = net worth less PCSV (HDWX) + retirement wealth (RW) .

Source: Author's computations from the 1983, 1989, and 1998 Survey of Consumer Finances.

and augmented wealth averaged about 15% to 25% that of households headed by persons with a college degree or more (Table 13). For high school graduates, the ratios were about a quarter to a third, and for those with 13-15 years of schooling they ranged from about 40% to 50%.

Among households headed by someone with less than 12 years of schooling, mean income fell by 11.9% in real terms for age group 47-64 but rose by 11.8% among the elderly. Mean wealth fell by 11.8% among age group 47-64 but grew by 4.4% among those age 65 and over. All told, augmented wealth declined by 32.7% among the younger of the two groups and by 8.1% among the older. Among high school graduates, average income fell for all age groups, while mean wealth declined by 11.5% for age group 47-64 but rose by 1.3% for age group 65 and over. Augmented wealth fell for high school graduates in all age groups. Among those with one to three years of college, mean wealth collapsed for all age groups, and mean income declined moderately. As a result, total augmented wealth fell among all age groups with 13-15 years of schooling. Among college graduates, mean income and wealth advanced for 47-64-year-olds but plummeted for the elderly. Yet overall, mean augmented wealth was down for both groups, by 3.1% among age group 47-64 and by 26.6% among the elderly.

A breakdown of retirement wealth by age and marital status (**Tables 14** and **15** and Appendix Table 14), reveals much higher pension holdings, Social Security wealth, and total retirement wealth among married couples than among singles. The average pension and retirement wealth among married couples is about double that of single males and about 2.5 to 3 times that of single females (Table 14). Differences in Social Security wealth among these three groups are less marked, with the Social Security wealth of both single males and single females averaging about half that of married couples.

Between 1983 and 1998, average pension wealth increased for both age groups among married couples and single males and among elderly single females but declined among single females in age group 47-64. However, Social Security wealth fell among married couples in both age groups and among both single males age group 47-64. Average retirement wealth advanced among married couples in both age groups, among single males in both age groups, and among elderly single females. It fell slightly among single females in age group 47-64.

The average income and wealth by age group among married couples is about double that of single males, and for single males it is about double that of single females. All told, the augmented wealth of married couples was about double that of single males and triple that of single females. Among married couples and single males, mean income, mean wealth, and augmented wealth improved over the 1983-98 period for both age groups; mean income fell slightly for single females age 47-64. Percentage gains were considerably greater for single males than for married couples and single females.

Appendix Table 14 illustrates similar trends for income, wealth, and retirement wealth among five-year cohorts of married couples and single males and females.

TABLE 14. Retirement wealth by family status, age 47 and over, 1983, 1989, and 1998
(in thousands, 1998 dollars)

Category	Mean value			Percentage change		
	1983	1989	1998	1983-89	1989-98	1983-98
A. Married couple						
All, age 47 and over						
Mean DC + DB pension wealth	$92.2	$112.8	$157.2	22.3%	39.4%	70.4%
Mean Social Security wealth	193.5	145.2	163.6	-25.0%	12.7%	-15.5%
Mean retirement wealth	285.8	258.0	320.7	-9.7%	24.3%	12.2%
Ages 47-64						
Mean DC + DB pension wealth	109.6	109.9	154.1	0.2%	40.2%	40.5%
Mean Social Security wealth	182.5	133.7	156.6	-26.7%	17.2%	-14.2%
Mean retirement wealth	292.1	243.6	310.7	-16.6%	27.6%	6.4%
Ages 65 and over						
Mean DC + DB pension wealth	60.1	117.5	162.4	95.6%	38.2%	170.3%
Mean Social Security wealth	214.1	163.9	175.4	-23.4%	7.0%	-18.1%
Mean retirement wealth	274.2	281.4	337.7	2.6%	20.0%	23.2%
B. Single male						
All, age 47 and over						
Mean DC + DB pension wealth	42.2	52.3	86.8	24.1%	65.9%	105.9%
Mean Social Security wealth	67.5	61.1	76.0	-9.5%	24.4%	12.6%
Mean retirement wealth	109.6	113.4	162.8	3.4%	43.6%	48.5%
Ages 47-64						
Mean DC + DB pension wealth	44.0	51.3	94.2	16.7%	83.6%	114.3%
Mean Social Security wealth	67.0	54.8	66.3	-18.3%	21.0%	-1.1%
Mean retirement wealth	111.0	106.1	160.5	-4.4%	51.3%	44.6%
Ages 65 and over						
Mean DC + DB pension wealth	36.3	53.7	74.9	48.2%	39.3%	106.5%
Mean Social Security wealth	68.9	69.5	91.6	0.8%	31.9%	32.9%
Mean retirement wealth	105.2	123.2	166.5	17.1%	35.1%	58.3%
C. Single female						
All, age 47 and over						
Mean DC + DB pension wealth	61.0	42.7	56.3	-30.0%	32.0%	-7.6%
Mean Social Security wealth	55.0	79.5	71.5	44.6%	-10.0%	30.1%
Mean retirement wealth	116.0	122.2	127.9	5.3%	4.7%	10.3%
Ages 47-64						
Mean DC + DB pension wealth	67.5	46.0	56.3	-31.8%	22.3%	-16.6%
Mean Social Security wealth	56.4	60.7	64.0	7.7%	5.3%	13.4%
Mean retirement wealth	123.9	106.8	120.3	-13.8%	12.6%	-2.9%
Ages 65 and over						
Mean DC + DB pension wealth	55.3	40.0	56.4	-27.7%	41.0%	1.9%
Mean Social Security wealth	53.7	92.2	77.3	71.5%	-16.1%	43.9%
Mean retirement wealth	109.0	132.1	133.7	21.2%	1.2%	22.6%

Note: Households are classified by the age of the head of household.
Key: Retirement wealth (RW) = DC pension accounts + DB pension wealth + Social Security wealth.

Source: Author's computations from the 1983, 1989, and 1998 Survey of Consumer Finances.

TABLE 15. Income and wealth by family status, age 47 and over, 1983, 1989, and 1998
(in thousands, 1998 dollars)

Category	Mean value			Percentage change		
	1983	1989	1998	1983-89	1989-98	1983-98
A. Married couple						
All, age 47 and over						
Mean income	$64.5	$70.4	$78.2	9.1%	11.0%	21.2%
Mean net worth (HDW)	474.0	536.0	583.2	13.1%	8.8%	23.0%
Mean augmented wealth	752.3	779.3	826.2	3.6%	6.0%	9.8%
Ages 47-64						
Mean income	72.8	81.4	91.3	11.8%	12.1%	25.4%
Mean net worth (HDW)	453.7	502.5	594.2	10.8%	18.3%	31.0%
Mean augmented wealth	736.0	724.7	814.0	-1.5%	12.3%	10.6%
Ages 65 and over						
Mean income	49.1	52.5	56.0	7.0%	6.5%	13.9%
Mean net worth (HDW)	511.8	590.4	564.4	15.4%	-4.4%	10.3%
Mean augmented wealth	782.7	868.3	846.9	10.9%	-2.5%	8.2%
B. Single male						
All, age 47 and over						
Mean income	31.0	33.9	41.8	9.3%	23.3%	34.8%
Mean net worth (HDW)	174.6	189.7	336.8	8.6%	77.5%	92.9%
Mean augmented wealth	282.6	298.7	457.6	5.7%	53.2%	61.9%
Ages 47-64						
Mean income	32.7	43.2	49.0	32.0%	13.4%	49.8%
Mean net worth (HDW)	168.6	209.3	282.5	24.1%	34.9%	67.5%
Mean augmented wealth	277.4	307.7	391.9	10.9%	27.4%	41.3%
Ages 65 and over						
Mean income	25.5	21.5	30.3	-15.8%	40.8%	18.6%
Mean net worth (HDW)	194.4	163.4	424.5	-16.0%	159.8%	118.4%
Mean augmented wealth	299.6	286.6	563.5	-4.3%	96.6%	88.1%
C. Single female						
All, age 47 and over						
Mean income	23.0	21.0	23.2	-8.4%	10.5%	1.2%
Mean net worth (HDW)	144.7	148.0	168.1	2.3%	13.6%	16.2%
Mean augmented wealth	259.5	267.3	280.8	3.0%	5.1%	8.2%
Ages 47-64						
Mean income	28.9	24.6	28.7	-15.0%	16.5%	-0.9%
Mean net worth (HDW)	119.0	131.8	158.2	10.8%	20.1%	33.0%
Mean augmented wealth	240.3	232.0	254.0	-3.4%	9.5%	5.7%
Ages 65 and over						
Mean income	17.7	18.6	19.1	5.0%	2.6%	7.7%
Mean net worth (HDW)	167.3	159.0	175.7	-5.0%	10.5%	5.0%
Mean augmented wealth	276.3	291.1	301.3	5.3%	3.5%	9.0%

Note: Households are classified by the age of the head of household.
Key: Augmented wealth = net worth less PCSV (HDWX) + retirement wealth (RW).

Source: Author's computations from the 1983, 1989, and 1998 Survey of Consumer Finances.

Tables **16** and **17** (and Appendix Table 15) show a similar set of statistics by homeowner status. Homeowners have about three times as much total pension wealth, about 50% more Social Security wealth, and about twice as much retirement wealth as renters. Homeowners in both age groups saw gains in their pension wealth and their total retirement wealth but declines in their Social Security wealth between 1983 and 1998. Renters in age bracket 47 to 64, on the other hand, experienced declines in all three kinds of wealth, while elderly renters saw a modest gain in pension wealth but declines in Social Security wealth and total retirement wealth.

TABLE 16. Retirement wealth by homeowner status, age 47 and over, 1983, 1989, and 1998
(in thousands, 1998 dollars)

	Mean value			Percentage change		
Category	1983	1989	1998	1983-89	1989-98	1983-98
A. Homeowners						
All, age 47 and over						
Mean DC + DB pension wealth	$89.0	$95.7	$135.2	7.5%	41.3%	51.9%
Mean Social Security wealth	150.4	124.9	133.6	-17.0%	7.0%	-11.2%
Mean retirement wealth	239.4	220.6	268.8	-7.9%	21.9%	12.3%
Ages 47-64						
Mean DC + DB pension wealth	106.8	103.4	143.4	-3.2%	38.7%	34.2%
Mean Social Security wealth	153.5	116.8	133.0	-23.9%	13.8%	-13.4%
Mean retirement wealth	260.4	220.2	276.4	-15.4%	25.5%	6.1%
Ages 65 and over						
Mean DC + DB pension wealth	62.9	86.2	124.9	37.0%	45.0%	98.6%
Mean Social Security wealth	145.8	134.8	134.3	-7.5%	-0.4%	-7.9%
Mean retirement wealth	208.7	221.0	259.2	5.9%	17.3%	24.2%
B. Renters						
All, age 47 and over						
Mean DC + DB pension wealth	47.5	40.1	46.8	-15.7%	16.8%	-1.5%
Mean Social Security wealth	100.7	78.3	85.7	-22.3%	9.5%	-14.9%
Mean retirement wealth	148.3	118.3	132.6	-20.2%	12.0%	-10.6%
Ages 47-64						
Mean DC + DB pension wealth	52.4	29.6	48.4	-43.5%	63.5%	-7.6%
Mean Social Security wealth	96.8	68.9	83.1	-28.9%	20.7%	-14.2%
Mean retirement wealth	149.3	98.5	131.6	-34.0%	33.6%	-11.9%
Ages 65 and over						
Mean DC + DB pension wealth	41.3	50.7	44.5	22.9%	-12.2%	7.9%
Mean Social Security wealth	105.7	87.8	89.4	-16.9%	1.8%	-15.4%
Mean retirement wealth	147.0	138.6	134.0	-5.7%	-3.3%	-8.9%

Note: Households are classified by the age of the head of household.
Key: Retirement wealth (RW) = DC pension accounts + DB pension wealth + Social Security wealth.

Source: Author's computations from the 1983, 1989, and 1998 Survey of Consumer Finances.

Homeowners earn two to three times the income of renters, have over seven times the net worth, and about four times the augmented wealth. Homeowners saw their income, net worth, and total augmented wealth expand over the period from 1983 to 1998, particularly during the 1990s. Renters in age group 47-64 enjoyed increases in both income and wealth but suffered a slight decline in aver-age augmented wealth; elderly renters saw declines in all three measures.

As shown in Appendix Table 15, homeowners of all age groups saw their income and net worth expand between 1983 and 1998, particularly during the 1990s. Each age group also saw its pension wealth and its augmented wealth grow but its

TABLE 17. Income and wealth by homeowner status, age 47 and over, 1983, 1989, and 1998
(in thousands, 1998 dollars)

Category	Mean value			Percentage change		
	1983	1989	1998	1983-89	1989-98	1983-98
A. Homeowners						
All, age 47 and over						
Mean income	$55.8	$57.3	$64.6	2.6%	12.8%	15.8%
Mean net worth (HDW)	430.2	448.8	514.9	4.3%	14.7%	19.7%
Mean augmented wealth	663.3	658.1	719.8	-0.8%	9.4%	8.5%
Ages 47-64						
Mean income	67.1	71.8	81.9	7.0%	14.1%	22.0%
Mean net worth (HDW)	431.3	456.5	555.2	5.8%	21.6%	28.7%
Mean augmented wealth	682.6	657.6	746.8	-3.7%	13.6%	9.4%
Ages 65 and over						
Mean income	39.2	39.4	42.8	0.5%	8.8%	9.3%
Mean net worth (HDW)	428.5	439.5	464.0	2.6%	5.6%	8.3%
Mean augmented wealth	634.9	658.6	685.8	3.7%	4.1%	8.0%
B. Renters						
All, age 47 and over						
Mean income	24.1	25.6	25.1	6.4%	-2.0%	4.2%
Mean net worth (HDW)	67.8	104.2	73.7	53.8%	-29.3%	8.7%
Mean augmented wealth	215.2	218.9	191.6	1.7%	-12.5%	-11.0%
Ages 47-64						
Mean income	28.5	30.8	30.2	8.2%	-2.2%	5.8%
Mean net worth (HDW)	47.4	90.2	67.7	90.5%	-25.0%	42.9%
Mean augmented wealth	195.1	183.0	183.3	-6.2%	0.2%	-6.0%
Ages 65 and over						
Mean income	18.4	20.2	17.8	10.1%	-11.8%	-3.0%
Mean net worth (HDW)	93.8	118.6	82.2	26.4%	-30.6%	-12.3%
Mean augmented wealth	240.8	255.5	203.3	6.1%	-20.4%	-15.6%

Note: Households are classified by the age of the head of household.
Key: Augmented wealth = net worth less PCSV (HDWX) + retirement wealth (RW).

Source: Author's computations from the 1983, 1989, and 1998 Survey of Consumer Finances.

Social Security wealth decline. Renters under age 70, on the other hand, experienced declines in income over the 1983-98 period, though renters of age 71 and above saw income gains. The net worth of renters in age groups 53-58 and 65-70 declined over this period, while the wealth of renters in age groups 59-64 and 71 and over increased. Pension wealth fell in age groups 53-58 and 65-70 but rose in age groups 59-64 and 71 and over. Social Security wealth declined among all age groups except 53-58. Overall, augmented wealth fell for every age group except 71 and over.

Retirement income

The final part of the analysis projects the future retirement income of today's workers. The analysis is conducted in three ways. The first considers only the current financial wealth holdings among a given group and assumes an income stream equal to 7% of the financial wealth holdings. (An income stream of this size starting at age 65 would fully deplete the wealth holdings of the average male age 65 by the time of his expected death, given a 3% real rate of return on his wealth holdings.) The second is based on the total marketable wealth and assumes an income stream also equal to 7% of current wealth holdings. The third adds expected pension and Social Security benefits at retirement to the income stream generated by a 7% real rate of return on total marketable wealth. Expected pension benefits are based on respondent estimates (see the appendix for details). Expected Social Security benefits are based on a projection of future earnings and an estimate of the corresponding PIA (primary insurance amount). The analysis covers the years 1989 and 1998.[2]

A few words should be said about the appropriate measure of retirement security. Previous analyses of income adequacy for retirees are split in their use of net worth versus financial wealth as the basis for capital income flows (see, for example, Bernheim 1992, and Engen, Gale, and Uccello 1999). Those who use the latter argue that only actual or imputed income flows from fungible assets should be included in the income concept, because housing is not a liquid asset. Households who sell their homes to augment their income will still have to pay for housing in the rental market. Those who use net worth, on the other hand, argue that a homeowner with an identical level of financial wealth as a renter is better off, since the household does not have to pay additional income for housing. Indeed, national accountants include imputed rent to owner-occupied housing as an additional form of personal income. Moreover, the Census Bureau, in its extended income concept, also includes imputed rent to owner-occupied housing (see, for example, U.S. Bureau of the Census 1990). This author is in agreement with the latter position, and in previous work on household well being has included an estimate of imputed rent to homes as part of household resources (see Wolff 1990 for details).

Table 18 shows expected mean retirement income using these three methods. On the basis of 1998 data, retirement income should average $25,600 among all households in the 47-64 age range on the basis of their financial wealth holdings in 1998. This represents a 28% increase over the $20,000 (also in 1998 dollars) similarly aged households could expect to receive in 1989. Projected retirement income based on financial wealth holdings alone increased for all age groups between 1989 and 1998, with the strongest gains accruing to those age 53 to 64.

Both non-Hispanic white households and African American and Hispanic households also experienced an increase in their projected retirement income on the basis of their financial wealth holdings. Gains are again stronger among the older age group (56-64) than among the younger one (47-55). Growth was much stronger for black and Hispanic households than for white households between 1989 and 1998, but the former groups still had a long way to go: by 1998, white households still had five times the retirement income of black or Hispanic households.

In terms of educational attainment, households headed by someone with a high school degree or less would all experience declines in their expected retirement income (compared to 1989) based on financial wealth holdings alone. Among those with one to three years of college, the older households would see their expected retirement income advance while the younger ones would experience a decline. The same pattern holds for college graduates. Average retirement income also rose among all three marital groups, with the largest increases occurring among single males. Homeowners also gained, while renters saw mixed results: age group 47-55 experienced heavy losses, and age group 56-64 saw a modest gain.

The patterns for projected retirement income are similar if based on total marketable wealth. Age groups 47-49 and 50-52 experienced a modest decline over the 1989-98 period, while those in the four older age groups enjoyed robust gains. Both non-Hispanic white households and African American and Hispanic households gained in terms of projected retirement income, and the growth was again much stronger among the latter group. The results by education, marital status, and homeowner status are almost identical to those based on financial wealth holdings.

The patterns change somewhat when expected pension and Social Security benefits are added to the income stream. Expected mean retirement income increases by 7% between 1989 and 1998, from $46,900 to $50,000. Projected retirement income declined over this period among age groups 47-49 and 50-52 but rose for all other age groups. Projected mean retirement income is about two and half times greater among non-Hispanic white households than among African American and Hispanic households, though average retirement income increased 50% among older black and Hispanic households between 1989 and 1998, compared to an 11% increase among older white households, no change among younger white households, and a 14% drop among younger black and Hispanic households.

Expected mean retirement income from retirement wealth and marketable wealth for married couples was more than twice as great as for single males and triple that for single females in 1998. Between 1989 and 1998, projected retirement income increased strongly among older married couples, older single males, and both younger and older single females, remained unchanged among younger married couples, and declined sharply among younger single males. Expected retirement income among homeowners was three to four times greater than among renters. Older homeowners and renters saw strong growth in expected retirement income between 1989 and 1998, while the younger households in the two groups experienced little change over the period.

Because wealth is unequally distributed, changes in average values over the 1989-98 period, illustrated in Table 18, may reflect changes for only a small proportion of households. **Table 19** uses a different criterion to assess income adequacy – the poverty line. (We assume for this analysis that currently married couples remain married at retirement, that single males and females remain single at retirement, and that none have any dependents.) In 1998, the poverty line for a single elderly person was $7,818, and for a two-adult household it was $9,862. Table 19 details the percentages of households with expected retirement income less than their respective poverty line on the basis of the three income methods outlined above.

In 1998, 66.2% of households in age group 47 to 64 had insufficient income generated by their financial wealth holdings alone to get above this threshold. However, this was an improvement from 1989, when 71.9% of households would have fallen short of this goal. The situation improves when total wealth holdings provide the basis for income; in this case, 53.9% of households in this age group would fall short of the poverty line in 1998. However, this represents a slight deterioration from 1989, when the comparable figure was 53.5% of households. Under the third method, which adds in expected pension and Social Security benefits to the income generated by wealth holdings, the situation improves substantially, with only 18.5% of households failing to meet the poverty threshold in 1998. There is again a deterioration from 1989, when the corresponding figure was 17.2% of households. Under the third method, changes between 1989 and 1998 are mixed by age group. The fraction of households failing to meet the poverty line threshold increased among age groups 50-52, 53-55, and 56-58, but fell among age groups 47-49, 62-64, and especially 59-61.

On the basis of counting in pension and Social Security wealth, only 12.8% of non-Hispanic white households would fail to pass the poverty threshold in 1998, compared to 43.1% of African American and Hispanic households. However, the fraction of white households falling short of this income goal increased by 4.0 percentage points between 1989 and 1998, while the fraction of black and Hispanic households declined by 6.6 percentage points. The increase was especially high for whites in age bracket 47-55, while the decline was particularly pronounced for blacks and Hispanics in the 56-64 age group.[3]

In 1998, only 6.6% of married couples would fail to meet this income threshold on the basis of their expected retirement income from wealth holdings and pension and Social Security benefits, compared to 46.0% of single males and 33.5% of single females. The fraction of households failing to meet the poverty threshold

TABLE 18. Expected mean retirement income based on wealth holdings and expected pension and Social Security benefits, age 47-64, 1989 and 1998
(in thousands, 1998 dollars)

	From financial wealth holdings only			From marketable wealth holdings only			From marketable wealth and expected retirement benefits		
	1989	1998	% change 1989-98	1989	1998	% change 1989-98	1989	1998	% Change 1989-98
A. By age class									
All ages 47-64	$20.0	$25.6	28%	$26.4	$31.2	18%	$46.9	$50.0	7%
Age: 47-55	19.8	22.0	11%	26.0	27.1	4%	47.2	46.2	-2%
Age: 56-64	20.2	30.9	53%	26.9	37.4	39%	46.7	55.7	19%
Age: 47-49	18.6	18.7	1%	23.9	23.3	-3%	45.0	42.8	-5%
Age: 50-52	21.6	22.5	4%	28.4	27.8	-2%	50.6	46.9	-7%
Age: 53-55	19.2	25.6	33%	25.6	31.1	21%	46.0	49.9	8%
Age: 56-58	17.4	26.3	51%	23.6	31.8	35%	41.5	49.5	19%
Age: 59-61	24.1	38.4	60%	30.6	46.4	51%	51.2	66.8	30%
Age: 62-64	19.2	29.0	51%	26.3	35.3	34%	47.0	51.8	10%
B. By race/ethnicity*									
1. Non-Hispanic white									
All ages 47-64	24.2	30.0	24%	31.5	36.1	15%	54.2	56.0	3%
Age: 47-55	23.3	26.2	13%	30.3	31.9	5%	52.9	52.2	-1%
Age: 56-64	25.3	35.2	39%	32.8	42.1	28%	55.5	61.4	11%
2. African American or Hispanic									
All ages 47-64	3.7	6.0	62%	6.5	9.1	39%	20.4	22.1	8%
Age: 47-55	3.2	3.8	19%	5.9	6.1	4%	22.3	19.1	-14%
Age: 56-64	4.2	9.8	134%	7.2	14.3	100%	18.2	27.3	50%
C. By education**									
1. Less than 12 years of schooling									
All ages 47-64	5.7	4.1	-29%	9.6	6.6	-31%	22.1	16.0	-28%
Age: 47-55	4.7	4.5	-4%	7.9	6.5	-18%	20.5	15.3	-26%
Age: 56-64	6.6	3.8	-43%	11.0	6.7	-39%	23.4	16.6	-29%
2. 12 years of schooling									
All ages 47-64	16.4	9.8	-40%	22.7	13.9	-39%	45.0	31.1	-31%

Age: 47-55	15.7	7.4	-53%	21.9	11.0	-50%	44.0	27.8	-37%
Age: 56-64	17.6	12.7	-28%	24.3	17.6	-28%	46.9	35.3	-25%
3. 13-15 years of schooling									
All ages 47-64	19.4	17.8	-8%	26.6	22.7	-15%	50.0	41.3	-17%
Age: 47-55	18.3	14.3	-22%	25.7	18.9	-26%	49.4	36.8	-26%
Age: 56-64	20.5	24.1	17%	27.7	29.3	6%	50.6	49.2	-3%
4. 16 or more years of schooling									
All ages 47-64	64.2	55.7	-13%	77.2	64.8	-16%	115.9	90.0	-22%
Age: 47-55	61.1	43.4	-29%	73.4	50.9	-31%	111.0	76.2	-31%
Age: 56-64	67.9	81.9	21%	81.8	94.4	15%	121.8	119.5	-2%
D. By family status									
1. Married couple									
All ages 47-64	27.5	34.5	26%	35.4	41.7	18%	62.1	66.6	7%
Age: 47-55	26.7	28.9	8%	34.4	35.4	3%	60.9	60.6	-1%
Age: 56-64	28.5	43.4	52%	36.6	51.6	41%	63.4	76.2	20%
2. Single male									
All ages 47-64	10.7	16.7	57%	14.8	19.8	34%	26.7	27.8	4%
Age: 47-55	13.0	15.0	15%	16.7	17.4	4%	30.3	25.6	-15%
Age: 56-64	9.2	19.8	116%	13.6	24.2	79%	24.5	31.8	30%
3. Single female									
All ages 47-64	5.6	8.0	44%	9.2	11.1	20%	18.4	20.4	11%
Age: 47-55	3.7	7.0	88%	6.6	9.7	46%	16.0	18.8	18%
Age: 56-64	7.5	9.2	24%	11.9	12.8	8%	20.8	22.3	7%
E. By homeowner status									
1. Owns a home									
All ages 47-64	23.9	31.6	33%	32.1	38.9	21%	55.9	59.7	7%
Age: 47-55	23.2	27.7	20%	31.4	34.6	10%	56.1	56.1	0%
Age: 56-64	24.6	37.0	50%	32.9	44.9	36%	55.6	64.7	16%
2. Renter									
All ages 47-64	6.6	4.9	-25%	6.4	4.9	-24%	15.7	17.0	8%
Age: 47-55	9.1	5.5	-40%	8.9	5.5	-38%	18.7	17.8	-5%
Age: 56-64	3.3	3.6	9%	3.3	3.6	9%	11.9	15.1	27%

* Asian and other races are excluded from the table because of small sample sizes.
** Households are classified by the schooling level of the head of household.
Notes: A 7% real return on assets is assumed for financial wealth and net worth.
Households are classified by the age of the head of household.

Source: Author's computations from the 1989 and 1998 Survey of Consumer Finances.

TABLE 19. Percent of households with expected retirement income less than the poverty line, based on wealth holdings and expected pension and Social Security benefits, 1989 and 1998

	From financial wealth holdings only			From marketable wealth holdings only			From marketable wealth and expected retirement benefits		
	1989	1998	% change 1989-98	1989	1998	% change 1989-98	1989	1998	% Change 1989-98
A. By age class									
All ages 47-64	71.9%	66.2%	-5.6	53.5%	53.9%	0.4	17.2%	18.5%	1.2
Age: 47-55	72.5	67.2	-5.3	51.8	55.9	4.1	16.0	19.1	3.1
Age: 56-64	71.2	64.8	-6.5	55.2	50.9	-4.3	18.6	17.5	-1.0
Age: 47-49	76.1	69.8	-6.3	59.1	58.5	-0.5	24.0	21.8	-2.2
Age: 50-52	72.8	71.4	-1.4	50.7	58.2	7.5	10.7	18.8	8.0
Age: 53-55	69.6	58.1	-11.5	47.3	49.1	1.8	14.4	16.0	1.5
Age: 56-58	77.1	72.2	-4.9	58.5	59.7	1.3	18.7	22.2	3.5
Age: 59-61	70.2	56.3	-13.9	56.5	38.0	-18.4	19.6	12.9	-6.7
Age: 62-64	67.2	63.0	-4.2	51.4	52.5	1.2	17.6	15.7	-1.9
B. By race/ethnicity*									
1. Non-Hispanic white									
All ages 47-64	66.1	61.5	-4.6	45.2	49.7	4.4	8.8	12.8	4.0
Age: 47-55	68.0	62.0	-6.0	44.1	51.0	6.9	7.8	13.4	5.7
Age: 56-64	64.2	60.8	-3.3	46.4	47.8	1.3	10.0	12.0	2.0
2. African-American or Hispanic									
All ages 47-64	94.2	87.3	-6.9	83.9	73.9	-10.0	49.7	43.1	-6.6
Age: 47-55	94.0	89.5	-4.6	83.7	79.8	-3.9	45.8	43.9	-2.0
Age: 56-64	94.4	83.6	-10.9	84.2	63.3	-20.9	53.9	41.8	-12.0
C. By education**									
1. Less than 12 years of schooling									
All ages 47-64	86.5	88.5	2.1	70.9	78.9	8.0	31.6	45.4	13.9
Age: 47-55	86.2	92.9	6.7	70.1	88.9	18.8	32.4	51.9	19.5
Age: 56-64	86.7	84.8	-1.9	71.5	70.3	-1.2	30.8	39.8	9.0
2. 12 years of schooling									
All ages 47-64	73.0	78.0	5.0	45.5	63.5	18.0	4.7	19.6	15.0

Age: 47-55	80.8	80.3	-0.6	47.3	68.9	21.7	5.8	23.1	17.3
Age: 56-64	58.9	75.2	16.3	42.2	56.7	14.5	2.7	15.3	12.7
3. 13-15 years of schooling									
All ages 47-64	65.7	67.3	1.7	48.5	56.5	8.0	4.5	13.3	8.7
Age: 47-55	67.4	69.0	1.6	48.3	58.3	10.0	4.0	15.4	11.4
Age: 56-64	63.7	64.4	0.7	48.7	53.2	4.5	5.1	9.4	4.4
4. 16 or more years of schooling									
All ages 47-64	34.3	43.8	9.5	18.1	30.9	12.8	0.9	7.1	6.2
Age: 47-55	32.9	47.8	15.0	18.6	33.5	14.9	0.3	7.1	6.8
Age: 56-64	36.0	35.1	-1.0	17.5	25.2	7.7	1.5	7.1	5.6
D. By family status									
1. Married couple									
All ages 47-64	67.3	58.9	-8.4	44.7	43.8	-0.9	5.5	6.6	1.0
Age: 47-55	68.4	60.6	-7.8	42.2	47.0	4.8	5.3	7.2	1.9
Age: 56-64	66.1	56.2	-9.9	47.6	38.7	-8.9	5.8	5.6	-0.2
2. Single male									
All ages 47-64	73.0	73.3	0.3	61.9	68.4	6.6	28.7	46.0	17.3
Age: 47-55	70.3	72.2	1.9	66.5	69.2	2.7	23.1	48.7	25.7
Age: 56-64	74.7	75.2	0.6	58.9	67.0	8.1	32.3	41.2	8.9
3. Single female									
All ages 47-64	82.7	80.7	-2.0	71.6	71.3	-0.3	41.3	33.5	-7.8
Age: 47-55	84.3	82.6	-1.7	72.6	72.4	-0.2	42.5	34.1	-8.4
Age: 56-64	81.1	78.5	-2.6	70.6	69.9	-0.6	40.1	32.9	-7.2
E. By homeowner status									
1. Owns a home									
All ages 47-64	66.5	59.7	-6.9	42.7	43.7	1.0	6.3	9.1	2.8
Age: 47-55	67.0	60.1	-6.9	39.5	44.9	5.4	6.4	8.6	2.2
Age: 56-64	66.0	59.0	-7.0	45.9	42.1	-3.8	6.2	9.9	3.7
2. Renter									
All ages 47-64	90.6	88.6	-2.0	91.2	88.6	-2.6	55.5	50.2	-5.3
Age: 47-55	89.9	87.7	-2.3	91.0	87.7	-3.3	46.5	49.4	2.9
Age: 56-64	91.5	90.6	-0.9	91.5	90.6	-0.9	66.8	52.0	-14.8

* Asian and other races are excluded from the table because of small sample sizes.
** Households are classified by the schooling level of the head of household.
Note: A 7% real return on assets is assumed for financial wealth and net worth. Households are classified by the age of the head of household.

Source: Author's computations from the 1989 and 1998 Survey of Consumer Finances.

TABLE 20. Percent of households with expected replacement income less than one half of current income based on wealth holdings and expected pension and Social Security benefits, 1989 and 1998

	From financial wealth holdings only			From marketable wealth holdings only			From marketable wealth and expected retirement benefits		
	1989	1998	% change 1989-98	1989	1998	% change 1989-98	1989	1998	% Change 1989-98
A. By age class									
All ages 47-64	89.3%	87.7%	-1.6	80.3%	80.6%	0.3	29.9%	42.5%	12.6
Age: 47-55	90.8	89.7	-1.2	83.3	85.6	2.3	37.0	47.9	10.9
Age: 56-64	87.7	84.8	-2.9	77.1	73.0	-4.0	22.3	34.4	12.0
Age: 47-49	89.2	91.9	2.7	83.3	87.3	4.0	41.5	54.2	12.7
Age: 50-52	91.0	87.7	-3.3	85.4	85.5	0.1	39.4	46.8	7.4
Age: 53-55	91.9	89.3	-2.5	81.5	83.6	2.0	31.6	41.2	9.6
Age: 56-58	95.8	87.2	-8.6	86.2	75.4	-10.8	26.1	43.4	17.3
Age: 59-61	86.0	86.4	0.4	73.5	69.5	-4.0	27.9	27.4	-0.5
Age: 62-64	82.5	78.9	-3.6	72.5	73.4	0.9	14.2	28.0	13.7
B. By race/ethnicity*									
1. Non-Hispanic white									
All ages 47-64	87.9	85.8	-2.0	77.0	77.8	0.8	26.1	40.3	14.1
Age: 47-55	90.2	87.3	-2.8	81.2	83.0	1.9	35.0	46.7	11.7
Age: 56-64	85.4	83.7	-1.7	72.6	70.5	-2.2	16.7	31.2	14.5
2. African-American or Hispanic									
All ages 47-64	95.3	95.6	0.3	91.5	91.4	0.0	43.6	52.7	9.1
Age: 47-55	94.0	98.3	4.3	91.4	95.7	4.2	45.3	56.3	11.0
Age: 56-64	96.7	90.8	-5.9	91.5	83.9	-7.6	41.7	46.3	4.6
C. By education**									
1. Less than 12 years of schooling									
All ages 47-64	93.0	92.0	-1.0	83.9	83.3	-0.6	37.7	48.6	10.9
Age: 47-55	92.9	94.4	1.6	85.0	89.2	4.2	48.4	61.0	12.6
Age: 56-64	93.1	90.0	-3.1	83.0	78.2	-4.8	29.0	38.0	9.0
2. 12 years of schooling									
All ages 47-64	86.4	91.6	5.2	79.2	84.6	5.4	25.5	40.9	15.4

Age: 47-55	90.4	92.2	1.7	84.1	90.1	6.0	28.3	49.0	20.6
Age: 56-64	79.3	90.9	11.6	70.4	77.7	7.3	20.6	30.9	10.3
3. 13-15 years of schooling									
All ages 47-64	89.5	91.3	1.8	80.2	84.2	4.0	20.2	42.4	22.3
Age: 47-55	88.6	91.9	3.3	81.0	85.9	4.9	29.4	45.7	16.3
Age: 56-64	90.5	90.1	-0.4	79.3	81.0	1.7	9.8	36.7	26.8
4. 16 or more years of schooling									
All ages 47-64	82.5	79.7	-2.8	71.5	73.2	1.6	19.8	40.7	20.9
Age: 47-55	88.1	84.7	-3.4	79.7	81.0	1.4	27.9	44.1	16.1
Age: 56-64	75.8	68.9	-6.9	61.8	56.4	-5.4	10.1	33.5	23.3
D. By family status									
1. Married couple									
All ages 47-64	88.7	87.3	-1.4	80.5	78.9	-1.6	24.2	37.3	13.1
Age: 47-55	90.3	88.9	-1.3	84.0	84.0	0.0	32.5	42.7	10.2
Age: 56-64	86.8	84.7	-2.0	76.3	70.9	-5.4	14.3	28.6	14.3
2. Single male									
All ages 47-64	86.4	86.4	0.0	76.6	82.3	5.8	25.5	62.4	36.9
Age: 47-55	80.3	87.4	7.1	74.4	82.7	8.4	27.0	64.0	37.1
Age: 56-64	90.4	84.6	-5.8	78.0	81.6	3.6	24.6	59.6	35.0
3. Single female									
All ages 47-64	92.3	89.5	-2.8	81.4	83.7	2.3	46.1	45.0	-1.1
Age: 47-55	96.0	93.1	-2.9	84.5	92.0	7.5	52.7	52.5	-0.2
Age: 56-64	88.5	85.1	-3.4	78.2	73.9	-4.3	39.5	36.1	-3.3
E. By homeowner status									
1. Owns a home									
All ages 47-64	88.1	85.3	-2.9	76.5	76.0	-0.5	23.5	39.5	15.9
Age: 47-55	90.8	87.6	-3.2	80.9	82.2	1.2	30.6	45.5	14.9
Age: 56-64	85.4	82.1	-3.3	72.0	67.7	-4.3	16.3	31.2	14.9
2. Renter									
All ages 47-64	93.5	96.1	2.6	93.5	96.1	2.6	52.1	52.8	0.7
Age: 47-55	90.8	95.7	4.9	90.8	95.7	4.9	57.2	54.9	-2.3
Age: 56-64	96.9	97.0	0.1	96.9	97.0	0.1	45.8	48.4	2.6

* Asian and other races are excluded from the table because of small sample sizes.

** Households are classified by the schooling level of the head of household.

Note: A 7% real return on assets is assumed for financial wealth and net worth.
Households are classified by the age of the head of household.

Source: Author's computations from the 1989 and 1998 Survey of Consumer Finances.

changed very little among married couples between 1989 and 1998, increased by 17.3 percentage points among single males (and by 25.7% among single males in the 47-55 age range), and declined by 7.8 percentage points among single females.[4] As for homeowners, 9.1% failed to meet the income goal in 1998, compared to 50.2% of renters. However, while the share of home owners falling below the income threshold rose over the 1989-98 period by 2.8 percentage points, the fraction of renters declined by 5.3 percentage points (and by 15 percentage points among renters in the 56-64 age group).

Another criterion with which to judge retirement income adequacy is the income replacement rate – the ratio of expected retirement income to current income. The projections in the next two tables are based on expected pension and Social Security income at retirement, as well as *current* holdings of wealth (i.e., they assume no further accumulations of wealth before retirement). The projections further assume a 7% annuity flow from the stock of wealth, including defined contribution pension accounts.

Using an income replacement rate of 50% (**Table 20**), 87.7% of households would fail to meet this goal in 1998 on the basis of their financial wealth holdings; 80.6% on the basis of their total wealth holdings; and 42.5% on the basis of their wealth holdings and expected pension and Social Security benefits.[5]

The fraction of households failing to replace half of their current income rose dramatically between 1989 and 1998, by 12.6 percentage points. Every age group except 59-61 experienced large increases in their share. The fraction of non-Hispanic white households failing to meet this goal in 1998 was 40.3%, lower than the 52.7% for black and Hispanic households; this difference is partly the result of the higher current income among white families than among non-white families. However, the proportion of both white and non-white households and of most other demographic groups (with the exception of single females and renters) failing to meet this income criterion grew sharply between 1989 and 1998.

Table 21 looks at additional income replacement ratios besides 50%. In 1998, 15.5% of households will have income replacement rates of less than 25% at retirement; 42.5% will have income replacement rates less than 50%; 61.2% will have replacement rates less than 75%; and 76.1% will have replacement rates less than 100%. Between 1989 and 1998, the share of households able to replace a given proportion of their income *decreased* across the full range of replacement rates.

The proportion of households failing to meet the 75% replacement rate was substantially greater for households in age group 47-55 than in age group 56-64 – 67.2% versus 52.3% in 1998. This difference held at every replacement rate. These results are partly a reflection of the lower wealth holdings of younger households. Yet, the share of households failing to meet the replacement rate test increased between 1989 and 1998 for both groups.

The share of households unable to replace a given fraction of their income at retirement was substantially higher among African American and Hispanic households than among non-Hispanic white households at lower replacement rates (under 50%) but comparable at higher replacement rates (75% and above). As noted

TABLE 21. Percent of households unable to meet expected income replacement rates, based on wealth holdings and expected pension and Social Security benefits, 1989 and 1998

	Income replacement rates, 1989				Income replacement rates, 1998			
	< 25%	< 50%	< 75%	< 100%	< 25%	< 50%	< 75%	< 100%
All ages 47-64	7.7%	29.9%	56.1%	73.3%	15.5%	42.5%	61.2%	76.1%
Age: 47-55	9.1	37.0	63.2	78.6	18.7	47.9	67.2	82.1
Age: 56-64	6.2	22.3	48.6	67.6	10.7	34.4	52.3	67.3
1. Non-Hispanic white	5.5	26.1	53.1	71.2	12.4	40.3	59.8	75.9
2. African American or Hispanic	11.4	43.6	56.1	71.4	19.5	52.7	60.4	73.3
3. Married couple	4.3	24.2	54.8	74.1	10.2	37.3	58.8	75.3
4. Single male	6.2	25.5	50.7	63.1	42.9	62.4	69.2	83.9
5. Single female	16.9	46.1	61.7	75.8	14.5	45.0	63.0	74.1
6. Owns a home	4.4	23.5	51.1	70.5	10.4	39.5	59.1	74.7
7. Renter	19.4	52.1	73.5	82.8	33.0	52.8	68.6	80.9

Notes: Households are classified by the age of the head of household.
A 7% real return on assets is assumed for financial wealth and net worth.

Source: Author's computations from the 1989 and 1998 Survey of Consumer Finances.

above, this pattern is partly a reflection of the lower incomes in the black and Hispanic community. However, the income replacement failure rate rose between 1989 and 1998 for both groups and at every replacement rate level.

In 1989, single females had the lowest income replacement rates, i.e., the highest failure rates. Married couples had slightly lower failure rates than single males at lower replacement rates but higher failure rates at higher replacement rates. In contrast, in 1998, married couples had the lowest failure rates of the three groups across the board. Single females were next, followed by males, with the highest failure rates. Between 1989 and 1998, the income replacement failure rate increased at all levels for both married couples and single males, whereas it generally went down for single females. Income replacement failure rates are also much lower for homeowners than for renters. However, whereas among homeowners the income replacement failure rate increased at every level between 1989 and 1998, it increased among renters only at the lower replacement rates and actually went down at the higher replacement rates.

IV. Conclusion

While the average retirement wealth of American households increased from 1983 to 1998, the increase was not even across demographic groups, and the typical household did not benefit from the increase. The mean retirement wealth of non-Hispanic whites older than 47 increased 12.2%, but older Hispanics and African Americans saw their mean retirement wealth decline 14.6%. The worsening inequality in the distribution of retirement wealth is most visible if we examine the trends among wealth classes. Mean retirement wealth declined between 1983 and 1998 for older households (age 47 and over) with a net worth less than $500,000 and was essentially unchanged for households whose net worth was between $500,000 and $999,999. But the mean retirement wealth of older households with a net worth greater than a million dollars increased 43.8%.

Over this period, traditional defined benefit pension coverage declined, from 68% in 1983 to 46% in 1998 for households in age group 47 and older. The mean value of these plans for this age group fell as well, from $74,000 to $62,800. The mean value of defined contribution pension wealth, on the other hand, skyrocketed for these age groups. By 1998, about 60% of households in age groups 47-64 held some form of defined contribution pension plan, as did about 40% of households in age groups 65 and older.

The rise of defined contribution pensions plans more than compensated for the loss of defined benefit pension plans over the 1983-98 period in terms of average values. Mean total pension wealth (the sum of defined benefit plus defined contribution wealth) increased by 47% in real terms between 1983 and 1998 among households age 47 and over. The share of households in these age group covered by one or the other of these plans also grew slightly, from 68.9% to 69.5%

Social Security coverage grew as well. By 1998, 97.7% of households in age group 47 and over had Social Security wealth, compared to 86.1% in 1983. However, mean Social Security wealth fell over the period by 11%, from $138,500 in 1983 to $123,100 in 1998. Still, mean retirement wealth (the sum of defined contribution pension accounts, defined benefit pension wealth, and Social Security wealth) increased by 10% over the 1983-98 period among households age 47 and over, and mean augmented wealth (the sum of net worth and retirement wealth) grew by 8.8%, from $555,800 in 1983 to $604,600 in 1998.

However, the story changes when we look at trends in median values. Among the same households age 47 and over, median retirement wealth dropped by 6.9%, from $184,200 in 1983 to $171,600 in 1998, and median augmented wealth fell by 8.9%.

Average expected retirement income among households in age group 47-64 in 1998, on the basis of both the income generated by wealth holdings and their expected pension and Social Security benefits, was $50,000. But there were marked differences among demographic groups. Most striking, however, is that, on the basis of projected retirement income in 1998, 18.5% of all households in age group 47-64 – a higher share than in 1989 – will be unable to generate enough income to cross the poverty line. Moreover, 61.2% of these households will be unable to replace at least three-quarters of their current income at retirement on the basis of their accumulated wealth and their expected pension and Social Security benefits. By this measure, retirement income adequacy has deteriorated since1989, when 56.1% of households would have been unable to meet this goal.

All in all, the share of middle-age families with expected retirement income shortfalls rose over the 1989-98 period, despite the fact that older Americans became wealthier on average over the 1980s and 1990s. The contraction of traditional defined benefit pension plans and their replacement by defined contribution plans appears to have helped rich, older American but hurt a large group of lower-income Americans. Since 1998, the stock market has declined sharply, and it may be the case that many older Americans are now in a worse position than they were in 1998 or than similar households were 20 years ago.

Appendix A:
Literature Review

To date, no studies have estimated the complete wealth holdings (including Social Security and pension wealth) and their replacement rates for the elderly and pre-retirement age groups as recently as 1998. Moreover, no study has looked at changes in the economic status of the elderly over the period 1983 to 1998. Data from earlier studies that cover only the wealth situation of the elderly up to and including 1992 show that, on average, households are inadequately prepared for retirement and that wealth is unequally distributed, indicating that a significant minority of households are falling well below the target retirement wealth levels.

The composition of retirement wealth has changed markedly over the past 20 years, as coverage by traditional defined benefit plans declined and coverage by defined contribution plans, such as 401(k) plans, grew. Further, there is some evidence that the rise in defined contribution plans did not displace defined benefit plans, even after 1992. These trends raise the possibility that the adequacy of retirement wealth for households grew as total retirement wealth increased. However, the empirical evidence derived from the Survey of Consumer Finances (SCF) on this question (discussed later in this study) suggests that, despite a rise in retirement wealth for many households, the adequacy of retirement savings for the median household declined.

Previous work has focused on just one or a few of the aspects of the adequacy of retirement income or wealth. For instance, a number of papers have presented estimates of Social Security and/or pension wealth. The seminal paper on this topic is by Martin Feldstein (1974), who introduced the concept of Social Security wealth and developed its methodology. His main interest was the aggregate level of Social Security wealth and its effect on aggregate savings and retirement patterns. In a follow-up paper, Feldstein (1976), using the Federal Reserve Board's 1962 Survey of Financial Characteristics of Consumers (SFCC), considered the effects of Social Security wealth on the overall distribution of wealth. He found that the inclusion of Social Security wealth had a major effect on lowering the overall inequality of (total) household wealth.

This author followed up Feldstein (1976) by examining the distributional implications of both Social Security and private pension wealth. These studies include Wolff (1987), which used the 1969 Measurement of Economic and Social Performance (MESP) database and was the first paper to add estimates of private pension wealth and examine their effects on the overall distribution of wealth. The paper showed that, while Social Security wealth had a pronounced equalizing effect on the distribution of "augmented wealth" (defined as the sum of marketable wealth and retirement wealth), pension wealth had a disequalizing effect. The sum of Social Security and pension wealth has, on net, an equalizing effect on the distribution of augmented wealth. Wolff (1988) examined the implications of including both Social Security and pension wealth for estimating the life-cycle model of savings; Wolff (1992) addressed the methodological issues in estimating both Social Security and pension wealth; Wolff (1993a, 1993b) extended the estimates of Social Security and pension wealth to the 1962 SFCC and the 1983 SCF; and Chernick and Wolff (1996) examined the levels of Social Security benefits and Social Security wealth on the basis of the 1989 SCF by age group, lifetime earnings quintile, and family structure.

The most recent work on the effects of Social Security and pension wealth on the overall distribution of wealth was conducted by Arthur Kennickell and Annika Sunden (1999), who based their study on the 1989 and 1992 SCF. They also found a net equalizing effect from the inclusion of these two forms of retirement wealth. Interestingly, they found that there is a negative effect of both defined benefit plan coverage and Social Security wealth on non-pension net worth, but that the effects of defined contribution plans, such as 401(k) plans, are insignificant. As far as we are aware, there are no estimates of Social Security and pension wealth available from the 1998 SCF.

Several papers have used the Health and Retirement Survey (HRS). Alan Gustman, Olivia Mitchell, Andrew Samwick, and Thomas Steinmeier (1997) found that, in 1992 among households in the HRS, pensions, Social Security, and health insurance accounted for half of the wealth for those age 51-61; for 60% of total wealth for those in wealth percentiles 45- 55; and for 48% of wealth for those in wealth percentiles 90-95. In a follow-up study focusing on the role of pensions in forming retirement wealth, Gustman and Steinmeier (1998) used data from the HRS to examine the composition and distribution of total wealth for a group of 51- to 61-year-olds. They found that pension coverage was widespread, covering two-thirds of households and accounting for one-quarter of accumulated wealth on average. Social Security benefits accounted for another quarter of total wealth. They also found that the ratio of wealth to lifetime earnings was the same for those individuals with pensions and for those without. They concluded that pensions cause very limited displacement of other forms of wealth.

Several studies have documented changes in pension coverage in the United States, particularly the decline in defined benefit pension coverage among workers over the last two decades. Laurence Kotlikoff and Daniel Smith (1983), in one of the most comprehensive treatments of pension coverage, showed that the proportion of U.S. private wage-and-salary workers covered by pensions more than doubled between 1950 and 1979. David Bloom and Richard Freeman (1992), using Current Population Surveys (CPS) for 1979 and 1988, were among the first to call attention to the decline in defined benefit pension coverage. They reported that the percentage of all workers age 25-64 covered by these plans fell from 63% to 57% over this period. Among male workers in this age group the share dropped from 70% to 61%, while among females it remained constant, at 53%. Among studies by William Even and David Macpherson (1994a, 1994b, 1994c, and 1994d), the

1994c study showed a particularly pronounced drop in defined benefit pension coverage among workers with low levels of education; the 1994d study showed a convergence in pension coverage rates among female and male workers between 1979 and 1998.

A related topic of interest is whether defined contribution plans have substituted for defined benefit plans. Leslie Popke (1999), using employer data (5500 filings) for 1992, found that, indeed, 401(k) and other defined contribution plans have substituted for terminated defined benefit plans and that the offering of a defined contribution plan raises the chance of a termination in defined benefit coverage. On the other hand, James Poterba, Steven Venti, and David Wise (1998), using HRS data for 1993, found that the growth of 401(k) plans did not substitute for other forms of household wealth and, in fact, raised household net worth relative to what it would have been without these plans.

Several studies have looked at the overall economic status of the elderly. Michael Hurd (1994) showed that the mean income of households age 65 and over increased sharply between 1970 and 1975 but only moderately from 1975 to 1987. As a fraction of the overall mean household income, average elderly income rose from 54% in 1970 to 61% in 1975 and then to only 63% by 1987. James Smith (1997), using 1994 HRS data, found that median financial wealth among white households age 70 and over was only $15,600; for white households age 51-61 it was $23,400; and for black and Hispanic households in the two age groups it was zero. Venti and Wise (1998), using HRS data for 1992, estimated a high degree of wealth dispersion among persons age 51-61, even after controlling for lifetime earnings.

A Department of Labor report issued in 2000 found that a large proportion of workers, especially low-wage, part-time, and minority workers, were not covered by private pensions. The coverage rate of all private-sector wage-and-salary workers was 44% in 1997. The low coverage for part-time, temporary, and low-wage workers appeared to be ascribable to the proliferation of 401(k) plans and the frequent requirement for employee contributions to such plans. The report also found important racial differences, with 47% of white workers participating but only 27% of Hispanics. Another important distinction was union membership, with 70% of unionized workers covered by a pension plan but only 41% of non-unionized workers. Moreover, pension participation was found to be highly correlated with wages. While only 6% of workers earnings less than $200 per week were involved in a pension plan, 76% of workers earning $1,000 per week participated.

With regard to income adequacy at retirement, most studies conclude that a replacement rate of 80% or so (see, for example, Engen, Gale, and Uccelo 1999) is sufficient. The rationale is that, once retired, families do not have the same need to save for retirement. Moreover, the overall tax burden is lower because payroll taxes are no longer paid and because there are extra income tax exemptions. In addition, work-related expenses for clothing and commuting are no longer required.

Bernheim (1997), using a simulation model based on survey data from ICR Survey Research Group, estimated that baby boomers would need to triple their savings on average to have an adequate income at retirement. Retirement savings alone would yield income replacement rates from 16.3% to 49.0%. Married couples, higher earners, and workers with pensions would have the highest replacement rates.

Moore and Mitchell (2000) used the 1992 wave of the HRS to estimate income adequacy. They found that the median household would have to save an additional 16% of earnings if it were to retire at age 62, and an additional 7% to retire at age 65, with adequate income. Actual savings rates fell short by about two-thirds of the level required to attain income adequacy at retirement. The study also found that shortfalls were substantially larger for single male and single female households than for married couples. Higher-income households were found to have lower replacement rates than lower-income ones (85% for the second decile compared to 58% for the 10th decile). This finding largely reflects the higher pre-retirement income of the higher-income households. In contrast, retirement saving adequacy rose with wealth level. The authors calculated a replacement rate of 49% for households in the lowest wealth decile and a 100% replacement rate for households in the top wealth decile. Black and Hispanic married households had a larger income shortfall than whites, and more education resulted in improved adequacy.

Gustman and Steinmeier (1998), also using the 1992 wave of the HRS, found large shortfalls in retirement savings in terms of income adequacy at retirement. They calculated replacement rates in the range of 41% to 89%, with an average of 60%, relative to lifetime earnings. Indeed, replacement rates were 33% or less compared to lifetime earnings for one-fourth of the population. They also found that replacement rates declined with lifetime earnings.

Finally, Engen, Gale, and Uccello (1999), using both the 1992 wave of the HRS and the 1983, 1992, and 1995 SCF), calculated that only half of all households would be expected to meet the 80% income adequacy target. The chances of meeting this income replacement rate rose with education, and were greater for whites than for blacks or Hispanics.

These last four studies taken together imply that a substantial fraction of the American population will fail to have adequate income in retirement. They also project greater income adequacy for married couples than for singles, for whites than for non-whites, and for the more educated relative to the less educated. This study finds similar results.

Appendix B:
Estimation of Pension and
Social Security Wealth

I. General methodology

The imputation of both pension and Social Security wealth is summarized below. Greater detail can be found in the following sections.

Pension wealth: For retirees (r) the procedure is straightforward. Let PB be the pension benefit currently being received by the retiree. The SCF questionnaire indicates how many pension plans each spouse is involved in and what the expected (or current) pension benefit is. The SCF questionnaire also indicates whether the pension benefits remain fixed in nominal terms over time for a particular beneficiary or are indexed for inflation. In the case of the former, the (gross) pension wealth is given by:

$$(1a) \quad PW_r = \int_0 PB(1 - m_t)e^{-\delta t}dt$$

where m_t is the mortality rate at time t conditional on age, gender, and race, and δ is the nominal discount rate, for which the (nominal) 10-year treasury bill rate is used; the integration runs from the current year to age 109. In the latter case,

$$(1b) \quad PW_r = \int_0 PB(1 - m_t)e^{-\delta^* t}dt$$

and δ^* is the real 10-year treasury bill rate, estimated as the current nominal rate less the Social Security Plan II-B assumption of 4.0% annual increase of the consumer price index (CPI).

Among current workers (w) the procedure is somewhat more complex. The SCF provides detailed information on pension coverage among current workers, including the type of plan, the formula used to determine the benefit amount (for example, a fixed percentage of the average of the last five years' earnings), the retirement age when the benefits are effective, the likely retirement age of the worker, and vesting requirements. Information is provided not only for the current job (or jobs) of each spouse but for up to five past jobs as well. On the basis of the information provided in the SCF and on projected future earnings, future expected pension benefits (EPB_w) are then projected to the year of retirement or the first year of eligibility for the pension. Then the present value of pension wealth for current workers (w) is given by:

$$(2) \quad PW_w = \int_{LR} EPB(1 - m_t)e^{-\delta t}dt$$

where RA is the expected age of retirement and LR = A - RA is the number of years to retirement. As above, the integration runs from the expected age of retirement to age 109.[6]

Social Security wealth: For current Social Security beneficiaries (r), the procedure is again straightforward. Let SSB be the Social Security benefit currently being received by the retiree. Again, the SCF provides information for both husband and wife. Since Social Security benefits are indexed for inflation, (gross) Social Security wealth is given by:

$$(3) \quad SSW_r = \int_0 SSB(1 - m_t)e^{-\delta^* t}dt$$

where it is assumed that the current Social Security rules remain in effect indefinitely.[7]

The imputation of Social Security wealth among current workers is based on the worker's projected earnings history estimated by a regression equation. The steps are briefly as follows: first, coverage is assigned based on whether the individual expects to receive Social Security benefits and on whether the individual was salaried or self-employed. Second, on the basis of the person's earnings history, the person's average indexed monthly earnings (AIME) is computed. Third, on the basis of existing rules, the person's primary insurance amount (PIA) is derived from AIME. Fourth, Social Security wealth for current workers is given by:

$$(4) \quad SSW_w = \int_{LR} PIA(1 - m_t)e^{-\delta^* t}dt .$$

As with pension wealth, the integration runs from the expected age of retirement to age 109.[8]

II. Methodology in the 1983 Survey of Consumer Finances

This analysis follows the methodology (with a few modifications indicated below for subsequent years) laid out in the 1983 Survey of Consumer Finances codebook. This allows consistency with the estimates of both pension and Social Security wealth already provided in the 1983 SCF. The computations of retirement wealth in 1983 followed the following steps:

A. Pension wealth
Total gross pension wealth consists of two main components.[9]

1. (Gross) present value of pensions from past jobs: the sum of the present value of past job pensions for head of household and spouse.

2. Gross present value of pensions from current jobs: the sum of the gross present value of current job non-thrift benefits for household head and spouse. Expectations data are used for calculations.

The procedure is as follows. Pension coverage is first ascertained for current jobs. There are five possible categories:

1. covered and vested, anticipates benefits.

2. covered but not vested yet, anticipates benefits.

3. covered but not vested yet, does not anticipate benefits.

4. not covered, anticipates will be. Age when expected to be covered is ascertained.

5. not covered, never will be.

For those who are covered by a pension plan or expect coverage, the person is asked how many distinct pensions plans he or she is covered by. For each plan, the age at which the pension benefits are expected to be given is then asked.

The actual expected annual retirement benefit is then determined by the following steps. First, the age at which the respondent will be vested in each plan is determined. Second, the age at which the respondent could retire with full benefits is ascertained. Third, the respondent is asked the nature of the formula used to determine the retirement benefits. There are six possibilities:

1. retirement formula based on age.

2. retirement formula based on years of service.

3. retirement formula based on meeting both age and years-of-service criteria.

4. retirement formula based on the sum or age and years of service.

5. retirement formula based on meeting either age or years-of-service criteria.

6. other combinations or formulas.

Fourth, the age at which the respondent could retire with some benefits is asked. The same six choices of the formula used was then given. Fifth, the age at which the respondent expected benefits to start is asked.

Seventh, the expected retirement benefit is computed depending on the type of formula. This consists of three possibilities:

(1) the annual pay in the final year of the job is computed. This variable, used in pension benefit calculations, is computed by projecting current pay to the year the respondent says he/she will leave the job or retire. Wage growth is assumed to have three components: (i) occupation specific (adjusted for

age) taken from the slopes in the CPS log-wage regressions (for high-income observations this is assumed to be zero); (ii) a Social Security Plan II-B assumption of 1.5% annual economy-wide real wage growth; and (iii) a Social Security Plan II-B assumption of 4.0% inflation.

(2)   In some cases, the respondent reported expected retirement benefits. This variable is the expected dollar retirement benefits in the first year of eligibility as answered by the respondent. For some observations the dollar amount was reported directly, but for others it was computed by multiplying reported benefits as a percentage times the calculated projected final wage. The variable is given as an annual amount except when a lump sum is expected (in which case the lump sum amount is given).

(3)   In some cases, the respondent reported expected retirement benefits as a percent of final pay. This variable is the expected retirement benefits in the first year of eligibility as answered by the respondents, expressed as a percent of their projected wages in their final year of work. For some observations the percent was reported directly, but for others it was computed by dividing the reported dollar benefit by the calculated projected final wage.

Eighth, on the basis of the responses above, the present value of pension benefits from each current and past plan applicable to both household head and spouse was then computed. This variable is measured assuming an annual (or lump sum) pension benefit as given above, starting in the year of first benefits. Benefits for that and each succeeding year are adjusted for the probability of death and are discounted back to 1983. Sex-based Social Security mortality tables are used to compute the probabilities of death (standard for each year). These are capped at 109 years. Spousal survival benefits are assumed to be opted for 75% of the time and are randomly assigned when appropriate. Spousal survival benefits are also adjusted for death probabilities. Benefits are discounted at the 1983 long-term U.S. government bond rate of 10.85%.

Ninth, pension wealth was also computed for those individuals currently receiving pension benefits from past jobs. This was based on the following responses: (1) number of years receiving benefits, and (2) amount of pension benefit pay received in 1982. For pensions already being received, the nominal value of the pension is assumed to be fixed, and is indexed to the year it started by the actual price changes observed as measured by the CPI. The present value of pension benefits from each job is then measured assuming an annual pension benefit as given starting in the year of first benefits (or 1983). Benefits for that and each succeeding year (adjusted for probability of receipt) are discounted back to 1983. Sex-based Social Security mortality tables are used to compute the probabilities of dying each year and/or living to receive any benefits. These are capped at 109 years. Spousal survival benefits are assumed to be opted for 75% of the time and are randomly assigned when appropriate. Spouse mortality tables are also used. Benefits are discounted at the 1983 long-term U.S. government bond rate of 10.85%.

B. Social Security wealth

The gross present value of Social Security benefits is defined as the sum of the gross present value of Social Security benefits for household head and spouse. The Social Security formula and current receipts are used for calculations.

Among current Social Security benefit recipients, the steps are as follows: first, the kind of Social Security benefit received was determined. The possibilities are:

1. retirement.

2. disability.

3. both retirement and disability.

4. other kind.

Second, the respondent was asked the number of years receiving Social Security benefits. Third, both household head and spouse were asked the amount received in 1982.

Among future recipients, the steps are as follows. First, both household head and spouse were asked to report the age at which they expected to receive Social Security benefits (zero if he or she does not expect benefits). Second, respondents were asked the age at which Social Security benefits were expected to start. Third, the number of years until the start of Social Security benefits was determined. Fourth, the respondent was asked the total number of years on Social Security jobs to current date. If this was not answered, then an estimate of Social Security coverage was used, summing over current and the three possible past jobs. Fifth, an estimate of future years on Social Security jobs was computed from retirement years indicated by head and spouse.

Sixth, data on number of years on Social Security jobs, wage rates for each known job, estimates of retirement dates, and dates of starting benefits were used as inputs to Social Security formulas to compute benefits. Seventh, estimates of Social Security benefits were provided. A calculated value was based on the current job wage. All persons were assumed to work continuously until their stated age of full-time retirement, and then part time until their stated age of final retirement. All persons were assumed to retire no later than 72 or age plus one if currently over 72. Persons not currently working and over 50 were assumed not to work again. Wages were calculated by projecting current wages by the same method used to calculate final wages. Wage growth was assumed to have three components: (1) occupation specific (adjusted for age) taken from the slopes in the CPS log-wage spline regressions; (2) a Social Security Plan II-B assumption of 1.5% annual economy-wide real wage growth; and (3) a Social Security Plan II-B assumption of 4.0% inflation. Part-time years (if currently working full time) were assigned wages equal to one-half the projected full-time wages or the maximum amount allowable for full benefit receipt allowed by Social Security, whichever was smaller.

Eighth, the Social Security AIME was used as the basis of computing the Social Security benefit base. The variable is the average covered Social Security earnings per month (including zeros) for all years from 1951 or age 22 (whichever is later) to age 60. These are indexed by a Social Security wage index to the year the respondent is 60. Years after 60 can be substituted at nominal value. The five lowest years are dropped before an average AIME is computed. These procedures are mimicked using the SCF data on job earnings and future retirement plans to estimate an AIME value. Past and current job wages are projected back (and forward) to estimate earnings for each known year of work. These projections assume within-occupation real wage adjustments as taken from the CPS regressions (see past/current job), and economy-wide productivity growth and inflation as occurred or as projected to occur under the Social Security Plan II-B. Other years of unknown jobs are filled in with terms from the closest known job to fill in the total number of Social Security covered years. Wages are then capped at the actual or projected Social Security maximum and minimum coverage amounts. The AIME was then computed using actual or projected Social Security wage indices. The variable is currently estimated for all persons projected to have future Social Security benefits.

Ninth, the Social Security PIA on an annual basis is the basis of the calculation of Social Security benefits. It is computed from the AIME. In 1982 the monthly PIA was computed as 90% of the first $254 of AIME plus 32% of the next $1,274 plus 15% of the amount above. Calculations here take account of legislatively planned changes in this formula. The PIA is currently computed for all non-receivers projected to have future Social Security benefits.

Tenth, the present value of Social Security benefits is then computed assuming an annual benefit as given by the PIA estimate and starting in the year of first benefits (or 1983). Benefits for that and each succeeding year (adjusted for probability of receipt) are discounted back to 1983. Sex-based Social Security mortality tables are used to compute the probabilities of dying each year and/or living to receive any benefits. These are capped at 109 years. Benefits are discounted at the 1983 long-term U.S. government bond rate of 10.85%.

Eleventh, spousal benefits are also assumed at 50% of the primary benefit if a spouse is present. However, this variable will be zero if no spousal benefits are expected (such as when the individual's own benefits are larger than their spousal benefits). The age at which spousal benefits begin is estimated. Spouse mortality tables are also used for these calculations. The age at which widows' benefits first could be drawn is also estimated. It is an estimate of the age at which the individual could start to receive Social Security widows' benefits upon the death of his or her spouse. This variable will be zero if widows' benefits could never be drawn. An adjustment is also made if it appeared that the recipient's benefits had been reduced because of work. Benefits are discounted at the 1983 long-term U.S. government bond rate of 10.85%.

III. Modifications for years after 1983

A few changes were made in the procedures for computing both pension and Social Security wealth. First, the regression equations used to compute future earnings was modified as follows: human capital earnings functions are estimated by gender, race, and schooling level. In particular, the sample is divided into 16 groups by the following characteristics: (1) white and Asian versus African American and Hispanic; (2) male and female; and (3) less than 12 years of schooling, 12 years of schooling, 13 to 15 years of schooling, and 16 or more years. For each group, an earnings equation is estimated as follows:

$$\text{Log}(E_i) = b_0 + b_1 \text{Log}(H_i) + b_2 X_i + b_3 X_i^2 + b_4 SE_i + \Sigma_j b_j OCCUP_{ij} + b_{10} MAR_i + b_{11} AS_i + \varepsilon_i,$$

where log is the natural logarithm; E_i is the current earnings of individual I; H_i is annual hours worked in the current year; X_i is years of experience at current age (estimated as age minus years of schooling minus 5); SE_i is a dummy variable indicating whether the person is self-employed or working for someone else; OCCUP is a set of five dummy variables indicating occupation of employment ((a) professional and managerial; (b) technical, sales, or administrative support, (c) service; (d) craft, and (e) other blue-collar, with farming the omitted category); MAR is a dummy variable indicating whether the person is married or not married; AS is a dummy variable indicating whether the person is Asian or not (used only for regressions on the first racial category); and ε is a stochastic error term. Future earnings are projected on the basis of the regression coefficients.[10]

Second, the 10-year treasury bond rate prevailing for each individual year (1989, 1992, 1995, and 1998) was used as the discount factor.

Third, mortality rates by age, gender, and race are used instead of by age and gender alone in the computation of the present value of both pensions and Social Security wealth.

Fourth, for consistency with 1983, the Social Security Plan II-B assumption of 1.5% annual economy-wide real wage growth is used, even though this seems too high in comparison with the actual post-1973 growth in annual earnings (which has averaged about 0.2% per year). The Social Security Plan II-B assumption of 4.0% annual inflation is used as well, even though this seems too high.

IV. Questions on work history

Following is a sample of questions on work history drawn from the 1989 SCF codebook that is used to calculate the earnings profile of both household head and spouse and to calculate the AIME for each:

1. including any periods of self-employment, the military, and your current job, since you were 18, how many years have you worked full-time for all or most of the year?

2.   not counting your current job, have you ever had a full-time job that lasted for three years or more?

3.   I want to know about the longest such job you had. Did you work for someone else, were you self-employed, or what?

4.   when did you start working at that job?

5.   when did you stop working at that job?

6.   since you were 18, have there been years when you only worked part time for all or most of the year?

7.   about how many years in total did you work part time for all or most of the year?

8.   thinking now of the future, when do you expect to stop working full time?

9.   do you expect to work part time after that?

10.   when do you expect to stop working altogether?

Appendix C:
Supporting Tables

APPENDIX TABLE 1.
Household income by five-year age class, 1983, 1989, and 1998
(in thousands, 1998 dollars)

	1983	1989	1998	Percentage change		
				1983-89	1989-98	1983-98
A. Mean income						
All, age 47 and over	$48.2	$49.7	$56.0	3.2%	12.6%	16.2%
Age: 47-52	58.7	76.9	67.5	31.1%	-12.3%	15.0%
Age: 53-58	62.4	60.3	74.0	-3.3%	22.7%	18.6%
Age: 59-64	53.1	51.7	69.5	-2.6%	34.5%	31.0%
Age: 65-70	45.9	37.9	50.0	-17.4%	31.9%	8.9%
Age: 71-76	28.7	40.9	35.3	42.6%	-13.8%	22.9%
Age: 77 and Over	22.8	25.3	28.3	11.1%	11.6%	24.0%
B. Median income						
All, age 47 and over	27.9	28.4	32.4	1.9%	14.1%	16.3%
Age: 47-52	41.8	46.0	49.0	9.9%	6.5%	17.1%
Age: 53-58	42.6	39.4	43.0	-7.3%	9.0%	1.1%
Age: 59-64	32.5	32.9	35.0	1.2%	6.5%	7.8%
Age: 65-70	23.2	20.2	26.0	-12.9%	28.4%	11.8%
Age: 71-76	17.0	21.0	21.0	23.9%	-0.2%	23.7%
Age: 77 and Over	11.5	17.1	16.0	49.0%	-6.4%	39.5%

Note: Households are classified by the age of the head of household.

Source: Author's computations from the 1983, 1989, and 1998 Survey of Consumer Finances.

APPENDIX TABLE 2.
Household income by three-year age class, 1983-98
(in thousands, 1998 dollars)

	1983	1989	1992	1995	1998	Percentage change 1983-89	1989-98	1983-98
Mean income								
All households	$46.9	$49.0	$49.7	$46.6	$52.3	4.4%	6.7%	11.4%
Age: 47-49	63.8	69.2	68.0	74.4	65.4	8.5%	-5.6%	2.5%
Age: 50-52	53.7	83.8	75.4	71.1	69.5	56.0%	-17.0%	29.4%
Age: 53-55	60.4	62.8	68.7	69.1	82.1	3.9%	30.7%	35.9%
Age: 56-58	64.4	57.0	66.8	72.8	66.3	-11.5%	16.4%	3.0%
Age: 59-61	51.3	55.1	66.3	49.8	77.3	7.3%	40.4%	50.7%
Age: 62-64	55.1	48.7	55.5	45.3	59.6	-11.6%	22.4%	8.2%
Age: 65-67	51.8	42.9	48.3	51.5	54.9	-17.1%	27.9%	6.0%
Age: 68-70	39.0	32.6	33.1	37.8	45.4	-16.5%	39.1%	16.2%
Age: 71-73	32.8	37.9	31.5	29.8	39.1	15.6%	3.2%	19.3%
Age: 74-79	24.2	34.2	32.6	28.2	29.8	41.2%	-12.7%	23.2%
Age: 80 and over	21.1	24.5	23.6	26.9	28.3	16.6%	15.2%	34.3%
Median income								
All households	33.1	31.6	30.3	32.1	33.4	-4.6%	5.6%	0.8%
Age: 47-49	45.8	42.1	45.3	44.9	50.0	-8.2%	18.9%	9.1%
Age: 50-52	40.9	48.6	48.8	40.6	46.0	18.9%	-5.4%	12.4%
Age: 53-55	40.9	44.4	44.1	41.7	51.0	8.6%	14.8%	24.7%
Age: 56-58	44.2	36.8	37.2	42.8	36.0	-16.7%	-2.2%	-18.5%
Age: 59-61	35.7	32.9	36.0	28.9	40.0	-8.0%	21.7%	12.0%
Age: 62-64	31.4	32.9	29.0	25.7	30.0	4.6%	-8.7%	-4.5%
Age: 65-67	25.3	21.0	20.9	21.4	29.0	-16.7%	37.9%	14.8%
Age: 68-70	22.5	19.7	19.8	21.4	23.0	-12.4%	16.6%	2.2%
Age: 71-73	17.0	18.4	18.6	19.3	23.0	8.4%	25.0%	35.5%
Age: 74-79	14.1	18.4	22.1	18.2	17.0	30.7%	-7.6%	20.7%
Age: 80 and over	11.5	18.4	12.8	16.0	16.0	60.6%	-13.1%	39.7%

Note: Households are classified by the age of the head of household.

Source: Author's computations from the 1983, 1989, 1992, 1995, and 1998 Survey of Cosumer Finances.

APPENDIX TABLE 3.
Household net worth by five-year age class, 1983, 1989, and 1998
(in thousands, 1998 dollars)

	1983	1989	1998	Percentage change 1983-89	Percentage change 1989-98	Percentage change 1983-98
A. Mean net worth						
All, age 47 and over	$338.2	$357.2	$365.5	5.6%	2.3%	8.1%
Age: 47-52	319.6	369.1	361.5	15.5%	-2.0%	13.1%
Age: 53-58	354.7	352.4	447.1	-0.6%	26.9%	26.1%
Age: 59-64	358.7	404.1	584.3	12.6%	44.6%	62.9%
Age: 65-70	465.7	435.0	471.4	-6.6%	8.4%	1.2%
Age: 71-76	276.9	341.3	407.0	23.3%	19.2%	47.0%
Age: 77 and over	230.1	282.0	282.4	22.5%	0.2%	22.7%
B. Median net worth						
All, age 47 and over	327.1	285.4	298.1	-12.7%	4.4%	-8.9%
Age: 47-52	82.6	123.1	94.3	49.0%	-23.4%	14.1%
Age: 53-58	114.8	116.9	103.0	1.8%	-11.9%	-10.3%
Age: 59-64	122.5	122.6	165.2	0.1%	34.7%	34.9%
Age: 65-70	120.3	85.9	140.3	-28.6%	63.3%	16.6%
Age: 71-76	83.8	147.8	139.6	76.4%	-5.5%	66.6%
Age: 77 and over	70.2	79.3	117.6	13.0%	48.2%	67.5%
C. Percent of households with zero or negative net worth						
All, age 47 and over	7.8%	8.6%	7.5%	0.8	-1.0	-0.3
Age: 47-52	9.0	9.6	13.4	0.6	3.8	4.4
Age: 53-58	8.7	8.1	9.8	-0.6	1.8	1.2
Age: 59-64	6.8	10.9	5.4	4.1	-5.5	-1.4
Age: 65-70	5.2	9.5	3.4	4.3	-6.1	-1.9
Age: 71-76	6.2	6.4	5.7	0.2	-0.7	-0.5
Age: 77 and over	9.7	6.1	4.3	-3.6	-1.8	-5.4

* Percentage point change for panel C.
Note: Households are classified by the age of the head of household.

Source: Author's computations from the 1983, 1989, and 1998 Survey of Consumer Finances.

APPENDIX TABLE 4.
Household net worth by three-year age class, 1983-98
(in thousands, 1998 dollars)

	1983	1989	1992	1995	1998	Percentage change 1983-89	1989-98	1983-98
A. Mean net worth								
All households	$212.6	$243.6	$236.8	$218.8	$270.3	14.6%	11.0%	27.1%
Age: 47-49	432.0	328.1	314.6	358.5	326.3	-24.0%	-0.6%	-24.5%
Age: 50-52	211.8	405.9	422.0	355.5	395.9	91.6%	-2.5%	86.9%
Age: 53-55	319.7	365.3	415.6	398.4	447.1	14.3%	22.4%	39.9%
Age: 56-58	390.0	335.2	503.5	411.3	447.6	-14.1%	33.6%	14.8%
Age: 59-61	334.5	437.6	486.0	406.9	649.7	30.8%	48.5%	94.2%
Age: 62-64	386.8	374.5	402.2	366.4	501.8	-3.2%	34.0%	29.7%
Age: 65-67	447.2	470.8	457.0	435.3	462.9	5.3%	-1.7%	3.5%
Age: 68-70	487.2	397.4	348.9	334.9	480.0	-18.4%	20.8%	-1.5%
Age: 71-73	341.9	305.5	405.4	347.0	439.6	-10.6%	43.9%	28.6%
Age: 74-79	232.4	306.8	324.2	286.7	349.7	32.0%	14.0%	50.5%
Age: 80 and over	197.4	314.1	277.5	311.2	265.4	59.1%	-15.5%	34.4%
B. Median net worth								
All households	54.6	58.4	49.9	48.8	60.7	7.0%	3.8%	11.1%
Age: 47-49	82.6	99.9	66.0	96.0	90.6	20.9%	-9.2%	9.8%
Age: 50-52	87.9	136.9	91.5	77.5	100.0	55.7%	-26.9%	13.7%
Age: 53-55	98.4	145.8	123.2	110.5	142.7	48.2%	-2.1%	45.0%
Age: 56-58	127.5	110.5	129.3	89.0	82.6	-13.4%	-25.2%	-35.2%
Age: 59-61	143.4	110.8	152.7	127.8	185.5	-22.7%	67.4%	29.4%
Age: 62-64	100.7	125.9	98.8	118.1	115.3	25.0%	-8.4%	14.5%
Age: 65-67	114.7	84.8	113.8	97.5	134.0	-26.0%	58.0%	16.9%
Age: 68-70	124.3	89.0	118.7	93.4	142.3	-28.4%	59.9%	14.4%
Age: 71-73	88.7	129.1	108.2	127.9	134.0	45.6%	3.8%	51.0%
Age: 74-79	83.6	114.2	150.0	102.8	132.0	36.6%	15.6%	57.8%
Age: 80 and over	53.0	96.9	71.2	94.1	118.9	82.9%	22.7%	124.5%
C. Percent of households with zero or negative net worth								
All households	15.5%	17.9%	18.0%	18.5%	18.0%	2.4	0.1	2.5
Age: 47-49	4.4	13.7	11.3	11.9	14.5	9.3	0.8	10.1
Age: 50-52	13.4	5.9	11.6	14.1	12.2	-7.5	6.3	-1.2
Age: 53-55	9.3	7.5	12.0	10.0	9.7	-1.8	2.1	0.3
Age: 56-58	8.0	8.8	9.8	8.4	10.0	0.8	1.2	2.0
Age: 59-61	9.7	9.1	5.5	7.6	4.1	-0.6	-4.9	-5.6
Age: 62-64	3.4	12.5	8.9	13.4	7.0	9.1	-5.5	3.6
Age: 65-67	6.0	12.1	7.1	8.9	2.3	6.1	-9.8	-3.7
Age: 68-70	4.4	6.8	10.0	7.5	4.4	2.5	-2.4	0.0
Age: 71-73	6.4	5.6	6.4	4.4	5.6	-0.8	0.1	-0.8
Age: 74-79	6.6	5.3	2.2	4.9	5.5	-1.3	0.2	-1.1
Age: 80 and over	11.4	8.4	6.2	4.6	4.0	-3.0	-4.4	-7.4

* Percentage point change for Panel C.
Note: Households are classified by the age of the head of household.

Source: Author's computations from the 1983, 1989, 1992, 1995, and 1998 Survey of Consumer Finances.

APPENDIX TABLE 5.
Household financial wealth by five-year age class, 1983, 1989, and 1998
(in thousands, 1998 dollars)

	1983	1989	1998	Percentage change 1983-89	1989-98	1983-98
A. Mean financial wealth						
All, age 47 and over	$260.6	$279.4	$330.8	7.2%	18.4%	26.9%
Age: 47-52	232.5	280.3	289.6	20.5%	3.3%	24.5%
Age: 53-58	264.1	262.5	368.2	-0.6%	40.3%	39.4%
Age: 59-64	264.7	305.9	480.1	15.6%	56.9%	81.4%
Age: 65-70	374.2	349.9	365.3	-6.5%	4.4%	-2.4%
Age: 71-76	212.3	242.4	307.5	14.2%	26.8%	44.8%
Age: 77 and over	176.8	219.5	198.7	24.1%	-9.5%	12.4%
B. Median financial wealth						
All, age 47 and over	29.8	37.2	48.6	24.8%	30.7%	63.1%
Age: 47-52	17.8	33.2	45.9	86.4%	38.5%	158.0%
Age: 53-58	39.3	38.1	48.5	-3.0%	27.2%	23.4%
Age: 59-64	43.2	47.0	83.8	8.7%	78.3%	93.9%
Age: 65-70	59.5	30.0	53.7	-49.7%	79.2%	-9.8%
Age: 71-76	29.2	50.6	48.6	73.2%	-3.9%	66.4%
Age: 77 and over	20.5	37.7	35.8	84.1%	-5.1%	74.7%
C. Percent of households with zero or negative financial wealth						
All, age 47 and over	16.4%	17.4%	14.4%	1.0	-3.0	-2.0
Age: 47-52	23.9	17.5	21.3	-6.5	3.8	-2.7
Age: 53-58	16.3	20.1	19.1	3.8	-1.0	2.8
Age: 59-64	14.4	19.1	11.9	4.7	-7.2	-2.5
Age: 65-70	10.5	19.5	11.3	9.1	-8.2	0.9
Age: 71-76	14.5	14.8	11.8	0.4	-3.0	-2.6
Age: 77 and over	15.7	11.7	9.1	-4.0	-2.6	-6.5

* Percentage point change for panel C.
Note: Households are classified by the age of the head of household.

Source: Author's computations from the 1983, 1989, and 1998 Survey of Consumer Finances.

APPENDIX TABLE 6.
Household financial wealth by three-year age class, 1983-98
(in thousands, 1998 dollars)

	1983	1989	1992	1995	1998	Percentage change 1983-89	Percentage change 1989-98	Percentage change 1983-98
A. Mean financial wealth								
All households	$154.3	$181.8	$180.5	$167.9	$212.3	17.8%	16.8%	37.6%
Age: 47-49	335.3	250.8	246.4	288.8	259.8	-25.2%	3.6%	-22.5%
Age: 50-52	133.9	306.8	340.6	281.7	318.7	129.2%	3.9%	138.1%
Age: 53-55	232.0	273.6	334.2	319.2	368.0	18.0%	34.5%	58.6%
Age: 56-58	296.5	247.5	407.2	335.5	368.9	-16.5%	49.0%	24.4%
Age: 59-61	241.1	343.6	387.9	325.0	535.9	42.5%	56.0%	122.3%
Age: 62-64	292.0	272.7	315.6	279.9	409.7	-6.6%	50.2%	40.3%
Age: 65-67	349.4	373.9	361.4	343.2	358.2	7.0%	-4.2%	2.5%
Age: 68-70	403.1	324.6	256.4	262.0	372.4	-19.5%	14.7%	-7.6%
Age: 71-73	268.9	223.6	321.8	267.6	353.4	-16.9%	58.1%	31.4%
Age: 74-79	172.9	221.6	235.7	202.5	249.5	28.2%	12.6%	44.3%
Age: 80 and over	153.0	248.0	205.6	242.1	181.8	62.1%	-26.7%	18.8%
B. Median financial wealth								
All households	11.8	13.9	11.7	10.6	17.8	18.0%	28.0%	51.0%
Age: 47-49	17.3	26.9	21.2	32.1	47.8	55.8%	77.7%	176.9%
Age: 50-52	20.9	37.4	34.0	26.6	43.0	79.1%	14.9%	105.8%
Age: 53-55	27.5	42.6	56.1	31.7	73.9	54.9%	73.6%	168.8%
Age: 56-58	54.4	35.5	54.8	34.8	41.6	-34.8%	17.1%	-23.6%
Age: 59-61	59.6	42.2	84.3	35.4	102.0	-29.2%	141.7%	71.1%
Age: 62-64	29.8	47.0	32.9	51.3	27.4	57.9%	-41.7%	-8.0%
Age: 65-67	47.4	32.8	41.9	20.8	69.9	-30.8%	112.8%	47.3%
Age: 68-70	63.9	28.9	38.8	40.6	41.7	-54.8%	44.3%	-34.7%
Age: 71-73	33.5	37.1	32.2	33.5	57.3	10.9%	54.2%	71.0%
Age: 74-79	25.0	41.3	60.1	22.6	37.9	65.4%	-8.2%	51.8%
Age: 80 and over	15.8	54.1	12.5	20.9	35.9	243.1%	-33.6%	127.8%
C. Percent of households with zero or negative financial wealth								
All households	25.7%	26.8%	28.2%	28.7%	25.7%	1.1	-1.1	0.0
Age: 47-49	23.3	19.8	26.1	25.2	21.6	-3.5	1.8	-1.7
Age: 50-52	24.6	15.3	19.6	31.4	21.0	-9.2	5.7	-3.6
Age: 53-55	20.2	21.7	17.8	17.9	18.8	1.5	-2.9	-1.5
Age: 56-58	12.3	18.0	22.7	20.6	19.5	5.7	1.5	7.2
Age: 59-61	18.4	20.8	12.4	22.1	7.9	2.3	-12.9	-10.5
Age: 62-64	9.8	17.6	16.7	19.2	17.1	7.9	-0.6	7.3
Age: 65-67	11.3	26.9	23.1	20.7	10.1	15.6	-16.9	-1.3
Age: 68-70	9.4	11.7	15.5	14.6	12.5	2.3	0.8	3.1
Age: 71-73	16.6	17.1	15.2	14.5	8.5	0.4	-8.6	-8.2
Age: 74-79	12.0	12.9	10.3	9.6	14.6	0.8	1.7	2.5
Age: 80 and over	17.8	10.0	15.3	9.0	7.2	-7.8	-2.8	-10.6

* Percentage point change for panel C.
Note: Households are classified by the age of the head of household.

Source: Author's computations from the 1983, 1989, 1992, 1995, and 1998 Survey of Consumer Finances.

APPENDIX TABLE 7.
Household homeownership by five-year age class, 1983, 1989, and 1998
(in thousands, 1998 dollars)

	1983	1989	1998	Percentage change 1983-89	Percentage change 1989-98	Percentage change 1983-98
A. Mean home equity						
All, age 47 and over	$82.7	$87.3	$87.8	5.6%	0.7%	6.3%
Age: 47-52	87.1	88.8	71.9	2.0%	-19.0%	-17.4%
Age: 53-58	90.6	90.0	78.9	-0.7%	-12.3%	-12.9%
Age: 59-64	94.0	98.2	104.2	4.4%	6.2%	10.8%
Age: 65-70	91.5	85.2	106.2	-6.9%	24.7%	16.0%
Age: 71-76	64.5	98.9	99.5	53.2%	0.7%	54.2%
Age: 77 and over	53.3	62.5	83.8	17.4%	34.0%	57.2%
B. Median home equity						
All, age 47 and over	$57.3	$52.6	$59.0	-8.2%	12.2%	3.0%
Age: 47-52	60.2	52.6	42.0	-12.6%	-20.1%	-30.2%
Age: 53-58	61.4	57.8	51.0	-5.8%	-11.8%	-16.9%
Age: 59-64	73.6	65.7	65.0	-10.8%	-1.1%	-11.7%
Age: 65-70	64.2	52.4	69.0	-18.5%	31.8%	7.4%
Age: 71-76	49.1	72.3	72.0	47.3%	-0.4%	46.7%
Age: 77 and over	32.7	38.9	60.0	18.9%	54.2%	83.3%
C. Homeownership rate (%)						
All, age 47 and over	75.9	75.8	76.9	0.0	1.1	1.0
Age: 47-52	77.2	73.1	71.2	-4.1	-1.9	-6.0
Age: 53-58	74.8	81.0	75.9	6.2	-5.2	1.0
Age: 59-64	79.6	77.2	81.7	-2.4	4.5	2.1
Age: 65-70	81.4	76.1	81.1	-5.2	4.9	-0.3
Age: 71-76	73.0	78.8	80.2	5.8	1.4	7.2
Age: 77 and over	67.6	68.1	76.5	0.5	8.4	8.8

* Percentage point change for panel C.
Note: Households are classified by the age of the head of household.

Source: Author's computations from the 1983, 1989, and 1998 Survey of Consumer Finances.

APPENDIX TABLE 8.
Household homeownership by three-year age class, 1983-98
(in thousands, 1998 dollars)

	1983	1989	1992	1995	1998	Percentage change* 1983-89	1989-98	1983-98
A. Mean home equity								
All households	$58.3	$61.7	$57.3	$50.9	$58.0	5.8%	-6.0%	-0.6%
Age: 47-49	96.6	77.3	68.2	69.8	66.5	-20.0%	-14.0%	-31.2%
Age: 50-52	77.9	99.2	81.5	73.8	77.2	27.2%	-22.1%	-0.9%
Age: 53-55	87.7	91.7	81.4	79.2	79.1	4.5%	-13.7%	-9.8%
Age: 56-58	93.6	87.7	96.3	75.8	78.8	-6.3%	-10.1%	-15.8%
Age: 59-61	93.4	94.1	98.1	81.9	113.7	0.7%	20.9%	21.8%
Age: 62-64	94.8	101.8	86.6	86.5	92.1	7.4%	-9.5%	-2.8%
Age: 65-67	97.8	96.9	95.6	92.0	104.7	-0.9%	8.0%	7.0%
Age: 68-70	84.2	72.8	92.5	72.9	107.6	-13.5%	47.8%	27.9%
Age: 71-73	73.0	82.0	83.5	79.4	86.2	12.3%	5.2%	18.1%
Age: 74-79	59.5	85.2	88.5	84.2	100.2	43.2%	17.6%	68.5%
Age: 80 and over	44.4	66.2	71.9	69.1	83.6	49.0%	26.4%	88.2%
B. Median home equity								
All households	29.5	25.0	23.2	20.3	23.0	-15.2%	-7.9%	-21.9%
Age: 47-49	60.7	38.1	40.7	38.5	40.0	-37.2%	4.9%	-34.1%
Age: 50-52	59.4	57.8	41.8	48.1	45.0	-2.6%	-22.2%	-24.2%
Age: 53-55	51.4	60.5	52.3	51.3	60.0	17.7%	-0.8%	16.7%
Age: 56-58	70.0	55.2	50.0	50.3	50.0	-21.2%	-9.4%	-28.6%
Age: 59-61	73.6	71.0	58.1	50.3	78.0	-3.6%	9.9%	5.9%
Age: 62-64	74.3	61.8	46.5	50.3	55.0	-16.9%	-11.0%	-26.0%
Age: 65-67	65.5	50.0	54.8	64.2	62.0	-23.7%	24.1%	-5.3%
Age: 68-70	57.3	52.6	52.7	53.5	80.0	-8.2%	52.1%	39.7%
Age: 71-73	49.1	51.3	58.1	64.2	70.0	4.4%	36.5%	42.6%
Age: 74-79	49.1	50.0	80.2	72.7	70.0	1.7%	40.1%	42.6%
Age: 80 and over	32.7	39.4	40.2	36.4	58.0	20.5%	47.1%	77.2%
C. Homeownership rate								
All households	63.4%	62.8%	64.1%	64.7%	66.3%	-0.6	3.5	2.8
Age: 47-49	80.8	66.9	75.3	72.5	73.0	-13.9	6.1	-7.8
Age: 50-52	73.8	80.6	76.4	80.5	75.1	6.8	-5.5	1.3
Age: 53-55	74.8	79.1	75.9	79.7	74.3	4.3	-4.7	-0.4
Age: 56-58	75.8	83.9	77.6	78.8	81.4	8.1	-2.5	5.6
Age: 59-61	75.7	73.8	80.7	87.7	85.3	-1.9	11.5	9.6
Age: 62-64	84.2	81.0	79.7	80.5	78.2	-3.1	-2.8	-5.9
Age: 65-67	81.0	73.0	85.2	79.1	82.9	-8.1	10.0	1.9
Age: 68-70	81.8	79.5	76.2	74.1	80.7	-2.2	1.1	-1.1
Age: 71-73	73.6	78.0	74.7	85.4	81.6	4.4	3.6	8.0
Age: 74-79	73.2	75.6	86.3	78.4	78.0	2.4	2.4	4.9
Age: 80 and over	63.9	65.0	68.3	65.2	76.2	1.0	11.2	12.2

* Percentage point change for panel C.
Note: Households are classified by the age of the head of household.

Source: Author's computations from the 1983, 1989, and 1998 Survey of Consumer Finances.

APPENDIX TABLE 9. Household pension wealth by five-year age class, 1983, 1989, and 1998 (in thousands, 1998 dollars)

	Mean value			Percentage change			Percent holding asset			Percentage point change		
	1983	1989	1998	1983-89	1989-98	1983-98	1983	1989	1998	1983-89	1989-98	1983-98
A. DC pension accounts												
All, age 47 and over	$5.0	$9.5	$53.1	90%	458%	959%	7.8%	15.9%	47.8%	8.1	31.9	39.9
Age: 47-52	7.9	17.5	51.8	121%	196%	554%	14.2	35.7	57.5	21.4	21.8	43.2
Age: 53-58	8.8	17.8	65.9	103%	269%	648%	14.1	35.3	61.2	21.3	25.8	47.1
Age: 59-64	6.0	12.8	104.8	113%	718%	1646%	8.3	13.9	57.9	5.6	44.0	49.6
Age: 65-70	1.9	3.2	54.5	63%	1619%	2700%	3.4	2.1	49.6	-1.3	47.5	46.2
Age: 71-76	2.5	2.1	38.2	-15%	1728%	1450%	2.0	1.9	35.4	-0.2	33.6	33.4
Age: 77 and over	0.3	0.0	8.2	—	—	3013%	0.1	0.0	14.0	-0.1	14.0	13.8
B. Gross (DB) pension wealth												
All, age 47 and over	$74.0	$72.9	$62.8	-2%	-14%	-15%	67.8	58.9	45.9	-8.9	-13.0	-21.9
Age: 47-52	66.0	43.2	35.8	-35%	-17%	-46%	67.6	54.5	38.9	-13.0	-15.7	-28.7
Age: 53-58	96.8	57.0	50.4	-41%	-12%	-48%	69.0	63.4	42.4	-5.6	-21.0	-26.6
Age: 59-64	96.4	111.6	88.1	16%	-21%	-9%	70.1	64.5	49.2	-5.6	-15.4	-21.0
Age: 65-70	73.6	114.9	101.2	56%	-12%	38%	72.7	64.6	55.6	-8.1	-9.0	-17.1
Age: 71-76	51.3	73.7	76.8	44%	4%	50%	62.1	51.0	49.9	-11.1	-1.2	-12.3
Age: 77 and over	38.0	32.0	52.6	-16%	65%	39%	62.6	51.7	46.1	-10.9	-5.6	-16.5
C. DC pension accounts plus gross (DB) pension wealth												
All, age 47 and over	$79.1	$82.4	$115.9	4%	41%	47%	68.9	65.0	69.5	-3.8	4.4	0.6
Age: 47-52	74.0	60.7	87.6	-18%	44%	18%	68.5	72.3	71.1	3.9	-1.3	2.6
Age: 53-58	105.6	74.9	116.3	-29%	55%	10%	70.3	75.3	74.1	4.9	-1.2	3.8
Age: 59-64	102.4	124.4	192.9	21%	55%	88%	71.1	68.7	78.2	-2.4	9.4	7.1
Age: 65-70	75.5	118.0	155.6	56%	32%	106%	73.3	65.1	76.1	-8.3	11.0	2.8
Age: 71-76	53.8	75.8	115.0	41%	52%	114%	63.6	51.1	65.8	-12.5	14.7	2.2
Age: 77 and over	38.2	32.0	60.8	-16%	90%	59%	62.7	51.7	51.7	-11.0	0.0	-11.0

Note: Households are classified by the age of the head of household.

Source: Author's computations from the 1983, 1989, and 1998 Survey of Consumer Finances.

APPENDIX TABLE 10. Household Social Security wealth by five-year age class, 1983, 1989, and 1998 (in thousands, 1998 dollars)

	Mean value			Percentage change			Percent holding asset			Percentage point change		
	1983	1989	1998	1983-89	1989-98	1983-98	1983	1989	1998	1983-89	1989-98	1983-98
A. Gross Social Security wealth												
All, age 47 and over	$138.5	$113.8	$123.1	-18%	8%	-11%	86.1%	98.8%	97.7%	12.7	-1.1	11.6
Age: 47-52	108.7	91.5	104.8	-16%	15%	-4%	90.7	98.8	99.6	8.1	0.8	8.8
Age: 53-58	138.6	102.4	123.5	-26%	21%	-11%	94.5	99.4	98.3	5.0	-1.1	3.9
Age: 59-64	174.1	124.0	151.0	-29%	22%	-13%	90.7	97.5	99.0	6.8	1.5	8.3
Age: 65-70	171.4	138.7	166.1	-19%	20%	-3%	85.1	99.0	98.5	13.9	-0.6	13.3
Age: 71-76	131.8	142.4	130.3	8%	-8%	-1%	75.9	100.0	98.3	24.1	-1.7	22.3
Age: 77 and over	89.5	88.8	84.3	-1%	-5%	-6%	67.8	98.5	92.1	30.8	-6.4	24.4
B. DC pension plus gross (DB) pension plus gross Social Security wealth												
All, age 47 and over	217.6	196.2	239.1	-10%	22%	10%	97.2	99.4	98.3	2.2	-1.1	1.1
Age: 47-52	182.6	152.2	192.4	-17%	26%	5%	96.0	98.8	100.0	2.8	1.2	4.0
Age: 53-58	244.2	177.2	239.8	-27%	35%	-2%	97.6	100.0	98.9	2.4	-1.1	1.3
Age: 59-64	276.6	248.3	343.9	-10%	38%	24%	97.5	99.3	99.0	1.9	-0.3	1.5
Age: 65-70	246.9	256.7	321.8	4%	25%	30%	99.8	99.0	98.5	-0.8	-0.6	-1.3
Age: 71-76	185.6	218.2	245.3	18%	12%	32%	97.4	100.0	98.8	2.6	-1.2	1.4
Age: 77 and over	127.7	120.8	145.1	-5%	20%	14%	94.1	99.2	93.8	5.0	-5.4	-0.4
C. Median (DC) pension plus gross (DB) pension plus gross Social Security wealth												
All, age 47 and over	184.2	143.3	171.6	-22%	20%	-7%						
Age: 47-52	139.6	123.8	150.0	-11%	21%	7%						
Age: 53-58	191.0	143.9	175.3	-25%	22%	-8%						
Age: 59-64	246.5	182.7	215.0	-26%	18%	-13%						
Age: 65-70	232.5	207.7	255.0	-11%	23%	10%						
Age: 71-76	154.8	168.3	183.0	9%	9%	18%						
Age: 77 and over	96.5	100.8	105.0	4%	4%	9%						

Note: Households are classified by the age of the head of household.

Source: Author's computations from the 1983, 1989, and 1998 Survey of Consumer Finances.

APPENDIX TABLE 11 (PART 1 OF 4)
Household pension and Social Security wealth
by three-year age class, 1983-98
(in thousands, 1998 dollars)

	1983	1989	1998	Percentage change* 1983-89	1989-98	1983-98
A. Mean (DC) pension accounts						
All households	$3.6	$8.3	$36.8	131%	343%	923%
Age: 47-49	11.0	16.4	46.3	50%	182%	322%
Age: 50-52	5.0	18.5	57.1	270%	209%	1042%
Age: 53-55	9.4	16.0	71.4	71%	345%	662%
Age: 56-58	8.2	20.2	60.7	145%	200%	635%
Age: 59-61	5.7	14.4	104.4	151%	625%	1723%
Age: 62-64	6.3	11.4	105.3	81%	822%	1566%
Age: 65-67	2.5	3.0	59.4	21%	1854%	2269%
Age: 68-70	1.3	3.3	49.8	156%	1407%	3763%
Age: 71-73	4.3	3.7	37.2	-12%	896%	773%
Age: 74-79	0.3	0.0	28.3	-97%	—	9145%
Age: 80 and over	0.1	—	5.1	—	—	8230%
B. Percent of households with (DC) pension accounts						
All households	10.9%	24.0%	48.8%	13.0	24.8	37.9
Age: 47-49	15.7	29.8	57.1	14.1	27.2	41.4
Age: 50-52	12.9	40.9	57.9	28.0	17.0	45.0
Age: 53-55	16.7	30.2	65.9	13.4	35.8	49.2
Age: 56-58	11.4	42.3	56.7	30.9	14.4	45.2
Age: 59-61	7.7	18.2	67.6	10.5	49.5	59.9
Age: 62-64	9.0	10.1	45.5	1.2	35.3	36.5
Age: 65-67	4.3	2.7	54.1	-1.5	51.4	49.9
Age: 68-70	2.4	1.4	45.2	-1.0	43.9	42.9
Age: 71-73	1.9	3.3	44.6	1.4	41.3	42.7
Age: 74-79	1.3	0.1	21.5	-1.3	21.5	20.2
Age: 80 and over	0.0	0.0	12.9	0.0	12.9	12.9
C. Mean gross (DB) pension wealth						
All households	$50.9	$40.5	$35.6	-20%	-12%	-30%
Age: 47-49	57.4	39.7	31.1	-31%	-22%	-46%
Age: 50-52	74.3	46.3	40.3	-38%	-13%	-46%
Age: 53-55	85.8	54.2	39.6	-37%	-27%	-54%
Age: 56-58	107.9	60.8	60.7	-44%	0%	-44%
Age: 59-61	78.8	92.3	102.3	17%	11%	30%
Age: 62-64	116.8	128.5	70.0	10%	-46%	-40%
Age: 65-67	73.7	106.3	115.1	44%	8%	56%
Age: 68-70	73.4	123.8	87.9	69%	-29%	20%
Age: 71-73	51.6	95.2	87.2	84%	-8%	69%
Age: 74-79	49.9	35.1	60.2	-30%	72%	21%
Age: 80 and over	30.5	37.3	52.2	22%	40%	71%

*Percentage point change for panels B, D, F, H, and J.
Notes: Households are classified by the age of the head of household.
Statistics for all households exclude some households under the age of 40 with incomplete information.

Source: Author's computations from the 1983, 1989, and 1998 Survey of Consumer Finances.

APPENDIX TABLE 11 (PART 2 OF 4)
Household pension and Social Security wealth
by three-year age class, 1983-98
(in thousands, 1998 dollars)

	1983	1989	1998	Percentage change* 1983-89	1989-98	1983-98
D. Percent of households with (DB) pension wealth						
All households	52.6%	49.0%	35.3%	-3.6	-13.7	-17.3
Age: 47-49	64.5	54.7	36.5	-9.7	-18.3	-28.0
Age: 50-52	70.5	54.3	41.2	-16.2	-13.2	-29.3
Age: 53-55	68.6	64.3	44.3	-4.2	-20.0	-24.2
Age: 56-58	69.5	62.1	40.6	-7.4	-21.5	-28.9
Age: 59-61	66.7	60.6	50.5	-6.0	-10.2	-16.2
Age: 62-64	74.2	68.0	47.5	-6.2	-20.5	-26.7
Age: 65-67	69.0	60.1	57.5	-8.9	-2.6	-11.5
Age: 68-70	77.0	69.4	53.8	-7.7	-15.6	-23.2
Age: 71-73	56.2	55.3	53.2	-0.9	-2.0	-3.0
Age: 74-79	69.5	47.8	48.4	-21.8	0.7	-21.1
Age: 80 and over	58.1	53.8	43.9	-4.3	-9.9	-14.2
E. Mean (DC) pension accounts plus gross (DB) pension wealth						
All households	$54.5	$48.8	$72.4	-11%	48%	33%
Age: 47-49	68.4	56.2	77.4	-18%	38%	13%
Age: 50-52	79.3	64.8	97.4	-18%	50%	23%
Age: 53-55	95.2	70.2	111.0	-26%	58%	17%
Age: 56-58	116.1	81.1	121.4	-30%	50%	5%
Age: 59-61	84.5	106.7	206.8	26%	94%	145%
Age: 62-64	123.2	139.9	175.3	14%	25%	42%
Age: 65-67	76.2	109.4	174.6	44%	60%	129%
Age: 68-70	74.7	127.2	137.7	70%	8%	84%
Age: 71-73	55.9	98.9	124.5	77%	26%	123%
Age: 74-79	50.2	35.1	88.5	-30%	152%	76%
Age: 80 and over	30.6	37.3	57.3	22%	54%	87%
F. Percent of households with (DC) pension accounts or (DB) pension wealth						
All households	54.4%	60.5%	64.6%	6.0	4.2	10.2
Age: 47-49	65.7	67.6	69.9	2.0	2.3	4.3
Age: 50-52	71.1	76.6	72.2	5.4	-4.4	1.1
Age: 53-55	70.4	73.9	79.0	3.5	5.2	8.6
Age: 56-58	70.3	77.2	69.4	6.9	-7.8	-0.9
Age: 59-61	66.8	66.3	83.1	-0.5	16.8	16.3
Age: 62-64	76.1	70.9	71.9	-5.2	1.0	-4.2
Age: 65-67	70.0	60.2	82.5	-9.8	22.2	12.5
Age: 68-70	77.2	70.1	70.0	-7.0	-0.1	-7.2
Age: 71-73	57.7	55.3	71.9	-2.4	16.7	14.2
Age: 74-79	70.5	47.8	58.6	-22.6	10.8	-11.9
Age: 80 and over	58.1	53.8	49.1	-4.3	-4.7	-9.0

*Percentage point change for panels B, D, F, H, and J.
Notes: Households are classified by the age of the head of household.
Statistics for all households exclude some households under the age of 40 with incomplete information.

Source: Author's computations from the 1983, 1989, and 1998 Survey of Consumer Finances.

APPENDIX TABLE 11 (PART 3 OF 4)
Household pension and Social Security wealth
by three-year age class, 1983-98
(in thousands, 1998 dollars)

	1983	1989	1998	Percentage change* 1983-89	1989-98	1983-98
G. Mean gross Social Security wealth						
All households	$117.1	$86.8	$98.6	-26%	14%	-16%
Age: 47-49	100.5	83.5	99.6	-17%	19%	-1%
Age: 50-52	116.6	98.7	109.8	-15%	11%	-6%
Age: 53-55	128.2	101.0	129.2	-21%	28%	1%
Age: 56-58	149.0	104.3	118.1	-30%	13%	-21%
Age: 59-61	170.1	112.7	146.1	-34%	30%	-14%
Age: 62-64	178.8	133.9	157.2	-25%	17%	-12%
Age: 65-67	191.0	138.5	184.3	-27%	33%	-4%
Age: 68-70	148.4	138.8	148.9	-7%	7%	0%
Age: 71-73	137.1	145.5	144.5	6%	-1%	5%
Age: 74-79	107.8	113.7	104.4	6%	-8%	-3%
Age: 80 and over	89.6	83.5	81.2	-7%	-3%	-9%
H. Percent of households with Social Security wealth						
All households	82.4%	99.2%	98.4%	16.8	-0.8	16.0
Age: 47-49	91.0	98.7	99.1	7.7	0.4	8.1
Age: 50-52	90.5	98.9	100.0	8.4	1.1	9.5
Age: 53-55	94.6	100.0	99.3	5.4	-0.7	4.7
Age: 56-58	94.3	98.7	97.4	4.3	-1.3	3.0
Age: 59-61	91.6	95.2	98.9	3.6	3.7	7.3
Age: 62-64	89.5	99.4	99.1	9.9	-0.3	9.6
Age: 65-67	90.3	99.3	97.8	9.0	-1.5	7.5
Age: 68-70	79.2	98.7	99.1	19.6	0.4	19.9
Age: 71-73	75.7	100.0	100.0	24.3	0.0	24.3
Age: 74-79	70.3	99.2	96.6	29.0	-2.6	26.4
Age: 80 and over	70.4	98.4	90.1	28.0	-8.4	19.7
I. Mean (DC) pension plus gross (DB) pension plus gross Social Security wealth						
All households	$171.6	$135.5	$171.0	-21%	26%	0%
Age: 47-49	168.9	139.6	177.1	-17%	27%	5%
Age: 50-52	195.9	163.4	207.2	-17%	27%	6%
Age: 53-55	223.4	171.2	240.2	-23%	40%	8%
Age: 56-58	265.1	185.3	239.5	-30%	29%	-10%
Age: 59-61	254.6	219.4	352.8	-14%	61%	39%
Age: 62-64	302.0	273.9	332.5	-9%	21%	10%
Age: 65-67	267.2	247.9	358.9	-7%	45%	34%
Age: 68-70	223.1	265.9	286.6	19%	8%	28%
Age: 71-73	192.9	244.4	269.0	27%	10%	39%
Age: 74-79	158.0	148.8	192.8	-6%	30%	22%
Age: 80 and over	120.2	120.7	138.5	0%	15%	15%

*Percentage point change for panels B, D, F, H, and J.
Notes: Households are classified by the age of the head of household.
Statistics for all households exclude some households under the age of 40 with incomplete information.

Source: Author's computations from the 1983, 1989, and 1998 Survey of Consumer Finances.

APPENDIX TABLE 11 (PART 4 OF 4)
Household pension and Social Security wealth
by three-year age class, 1983-98
(in thousands, 1998 dollars)

	1983	1989	1998	Percentage change* 1983-89	1989-98	1983-98
J. Percent of households with DC pensions or DB pensions or Social Security wealth						
All households	93.1%	99.6%	98.7%	6.5	-0.9	5.6
Age: 47-49	97.0	98.7	100.0	1.8	1.2	3.0
Age: 50-52	95.1	98.9	100.0	3.7	1.1	4.9
Age: 53-55	95.5	100.0	99.3	4.5	-0.7	3.8
Age: 56-58	99.6	100.0	98.5	0.4	-1.5	-1.1
Age: 59-61	96.7	98.6	98.9	1.9	0.3	2.2
Age: 62-64	98.4	100.0	99.1	1.6	-0.9	0.7
Age: 65-67	99.6	99.3	97.8	-0.3	-1.5	-1.8
Age: 68-70	100.0	98.7	99.1	-1.3	0.4	-0.9
Age: 71-73	97.5	100.0	100.0	2.5	0.0	2.5
Age: 74-79	94.9	100.0	97.3	5.1	-2.7	2.4
Age: 80 and over	95.4	98.4	92.5	3.0	-6.0	-2.9
K. Median (DC) pension plus gross (DB) pension plus gross Social Security wealth						
All households	$146.3	$93.3	$115.0	-36%	23%	-21%
Age: 47-49	126.0	110.4	130.0	-12%	18%	3%
Age: 50-52	160.8	132.8	164.0	-17%	24%	2%
Age: 53-55	176.5	144.6	204.0	-18%	41%	16%
Age: 56-58	207.3	143.9	150.0	-31%	4%	-28%
Age: 59-61	243.0	157.1	215.0	-35%	37%	-12%
Age: 62-64	257.0	216.9	235.0	-16%	8%	-9%
Age: 65-67	246.6	199.8	320.0	-19%	60%	30%
Age: 68-70	202.8	214.3	230.0	6%	7%	13%
Age: 71-73	166.4	172.9	220.0	4%	27%	32%
Age: 74-79	136.3	128.8	145.0	-6%	13%	6%
Age: 80 and over	88.1	102.5	102.5	16%	0%	16%

*Percentage point change for panels B, D, F, H, and J.
Notes: Households are classified by the age of the head of household.
Statistics for all households exclude some households under the age of 40 with incomplete information.

Source: Author's computations from the 1983, 1989, and 1998 Survey of Consumer Finances.

APPENDIX TABLE 12 (PART 1 OF 2)
Household income and wealth by race/ethnicity and age class, 1983-98
(in thousands, 1998 dollars)

	1983	1989	1998	Percentage change 1983-89	1989-98	1983-98
A. Non-Hispanic white						
1. Age: 53-58						
Mean income	$69.8	$67.9	$82.7	-2.8%	21.8%	18.4%
Mean net worth (HDW)	419.2	408.3	508.1	-2.6%	24.4%	21.2%
Mean financial wealth	317.0	306.6	421.6	-3.3%	37.5%	33.0%
Mean home equity	102.2	101.8	86.6	-0.4%	-15.0%	-15.3%
Mean (DC) pension accounts	10.6	21.1	70.7	98.7%	235.3%	566.2%
Mean (DB) pension wealth	104.8	64.0	52.1	-39.0%	-18.6%	-50.3%
Mean Social Security wealth	148.2	107.6	130.1	-27.4%	20.9%	-12.2%
Mean retirement wealth	263.6	192.7	252.8	-26.9%	31.2%	-4.1%
Mean augmented wealth	672.2	579.9	690.3	-13.7%	19.0%	2.7%
2. Age: 59-64						
Mean income	58.2	59.9	75.7	3.0%	26.4%	30.2%
Mean net worth (HDW)	405.2	482.2	654.9	19.0%	35.8%	61.6%
Mean financial wealth	304.8	373.2	544.7	22.4%	45.9%	78.7%
Mean home equity	100.4	108.9	110.2	8.5%	1.2%	9.8%
Mean (DC) pension accounts	6.6	15.0	115.4	126.4%	666.5%	1635.3%
Mean (DB) pension wealth	102.6	131.1	94.8	27.9%	-27.7%	-7.6%
Mean Social Security wealth	181.7	136.6	162.8	-24.8%	19.2%	-10.4%
Mean retirement wealth	290.9	282.8	372.9	-2.8%	31.9%	28.2%
Mean augmented wealth	689.5	749.9	912.5	8.8%	21.7%	32.4%
3. Age: 65-70						
Mean income	48.6	42.8	53.0	-11.8%	23.8%	9.2%
Mean net worth (HDW)	497.5	516.6	524.8	3.8%	1.6%	5.5%
Mean financial wealth	404.0	419.3	409.6	3.8%	-2.3%	1.4%
Mean home equity	93.5	97.2	115.2	4.1%	18.5%	23.3%
Mean (DC) pension accounts	1.7	3.7	62.8	121.4%	1582.4%	3624.4%
Mean (DB) pension wealth	78.2	107.8	103.2	37.9%	-4.3%	32.0%
Mean Social Security wealth	175.7	149.2	178.2	-15.1%	19.4%	1.5%
Mean retirement wealth	255.5	260.8	344.2	2.0%	32.0%	34.7%
Mean augmented wealth	751.3	773.6	806.2	3.0%	4.2%	7.3%
4. Age: 71 and over						
Mean income	28.4	36.2	33.8	27.2%	-6.6%	18.8%
Mean net worth (HDW)	295.7	365.8	372.1	23.7%	1.7%	25.8%
Mean financial wealth	229.0	278.0	273.6	21.4%	-1.6%	19.5%
Mean home equity	66.7	87.8	98.5	31.7%	12.1%	47.6%
Mean (DC) pension accounts	1.6	1.2	23.4	-29.7%	1932.6%	1329.8%
Mean (DB) pension wealth	48.2	55.9	67.4	15.9%	20.5%	39.7%
Mean Social Security wealth	114.5	120.9	110.3	5.6%	-8.8%	-3.7%
Mean retirement wealth	164.4	178.0	201.2	8.3%	13.0%	22.4%
Mean augmented wealth	458.5	542.7	549.8	18.4%	1.3%	19.9%

Notes: Households are classified by the age of the head of household. Asian and other races are excluded from the table because of small sample sizes.
Key:
1. Retirement wealth = DC pension accounts + gross DB pension wealth + Social Security wealth.
2. Augmented wealth = net worth (HDW) + retirement wealth.

Source: Author's computations from the 1983, 1989, and 1998 Survey of Consumer Finances.

APPENDIX TABLE 12 (PART 2 OF 2)
Household income and wealth by race/ethnicity and age class, 1983-98
(in thousands, 1998 dollars)

	1983	1989	1998	Percentage change		
				1983-89	1989-98	1983-98
B. African American or Hispanic						
1. Age: 53-58						
Mean income	$22.1	$21.4	$27.7	-3.2%	29.3%	25.2%
Mean net worth (HDW)	71.1	81.1	132.8	14.0%	63.7%	86.7%
Mean financial wealth	32.7	41.9	87.7	27.9%	109.5%	168.0%
Mean home equity	38.4	39.3	45.1	2.3%	14.7%	17.3%
Mean (DC) pension accounts	1.5	2.9	14.8	88.8%	416.7%	875.3%
Mean (DB) pension wealth	63.1	41.4	45.7	-34.4%	10.4%	-27.6%
Mean Social Security wealth	100.6	61.1	88.4	-39.3%	44.7%	-12.2%
Mean retirement wealth	165.3	105.4	148.9	-36.2%	41.3%	-9.9%
Mean augmented wealth	234.9	183.6	266.9	-21.8%	45.3%	13.6%
2. Age: 59-64						
Mean income	18.2	17.0	24.2	-6.6%	42.0%	32.7%
Mean net worth (HDW)	69.3	70.0	113.3	1.0%	61.9%	63.5%
Mean financial wealth	32.4	31.6	68.9	-2.2%	117.6%	112.8%
Mean home equity	36.9	38.4	44.5	3.8%	15.9%	20.3%
Mean (DC) pension accounts	2.0	1.6	7.7	-20.1%	379.0%	282.9%
Mean (DB) pension wealth	77.1	42.7	51.1	-44.6%	19.7%	-33.7%
Mean Social Security wealth	136.7	59.1	82.6	-56.8%	39.9%	-39.6%
Mean retirement wealth	215.9	103.4	141.5	-52.1%	36.9%	-34.5%
Mean augmented wealth	283.2	171.8	247.1	-39.3%	43.8%	-12.8%
3. Age: 65-70						
Mean income	14.8	15.4	20.9	4.0%	35.8%	41.3%
Mean net worth (HDW)	73.1	46.3	94.0	-36.7%	103.1%	28.6%
Mean financial wealth	41.4	13.4	60.1	-67.7%	349.1%	45.0%
Mean home equity	31.6	32.9	33.9	3.9%	2.9%	7.0%
Mean (DC) pension accounts	1.4	-	3.3	—	—	141.0%
Mean (DB) pension wealth	37.3	80.1	94.1	114.8%	17.4%	152.3%
Mean Social Security wealth	127.4	79.4	90.6	-37.7%	14.0%	-28.9%
Mean retirement wealth	166.1	159.5	188.0	-3.9%	17.8%	13.2%
Mean augmented wealth	237.8	205.8	278.6	-13.4%	35.4%	17.2%
4. Age: 71 and over						
Mean income	11.6	15.4	12.3	32.4%	-20.1%	5.7%
Mean net worth (HDW)	28.4	51.9	54.9	82.4%	5.7%	92.8%
Mean financial wealth	11.1	15.2	23.9	36.4%	57.1%	114.3%
Mean home equity	17.3	36.7	31.0	112.0%	-15.6%	79.0%
Mean (DC) pension accounts	-	-	0.3	—	—	—
Mean (DB) pension wealth	26.7	26.3	29.8	-1.2%	13.4%	12.0%
Mean Social Security wealth	89.7	68.4	55.8	-23.7%	-18.5%	-37.8%
Mean retirement wealth	116.3	94.7	85.9	-18.6%	-9.4%	-26.2%
Mean augmented wealth	144.8	146.6	140.5	1.3%	-4.2%	-3.0%

Notes: Households are classified by the age of the head of household. Asian and other races are excluded from the table because of small sample sizes.
Key:
1. Retirement wealth = DC pension accounts + gross DB pension wealth + Social Security wealth.
2. Augmented wealth = net worth (HDW) + retirement wealth.

Source: Author's computations from the 1983, 1989, and 1998 Survey of Consumer Finances.

APPENDIX TABLE 13 (PART 1 OF 4)
Household income and wealth by education and age class, 1983-98
(in thousands, 1998 dollars)

	1983	1989	1998	Percentage change 1983-89	1989-98	1983-98
A. Less than 12 years of schooling						
1. Age: 53-58						
Mean income	$31.2	$30.5	$27.5	-2.3%	-9.9%	-11.9%
Mean net worth (HDW)	111.2	117.6	134.8	5.7%	14.6%	21.2%
Mean financial wealth	62.6	61.5	91.0	-1.8%	48.1%	45.4%
Mean home equity	48.6	56.1	43.8	15.5%	-22.0%	-9.9%
Mean (DC) pension accounts	0.4	3.3	12.6	653%	280%	2760%
Mean (DB) pension wealth	45.8	29.6	23.8	-35.4%	-19.8%	-48.1%
Mean Social Security wealth	118.5	71.5	67.6	-39.6%	-5.4%	-42.9%
Mean retirement wealth	164.7	104.5	104.0	-36.6%	-0.4%	-36.8%
Mean augmented wealth	275.5	218.7	226.2	-20.6%	3.4%	-17.9%
2. Age: 59-64						
Mean income	26.5	28.1	20.6	6.1%	-26.6%	-22.2%
Mean net worth (HDW)	116.7	180.0	91.9	54.2%	-48.9%	-21.2%
Mean financial wealth	62.9	114.3	51.1	81.6%	-55.3%	-18.7%
Mean home equity	53.8	65.7	40.8	22.2%	-37.9%	-24.1%
Mean (DC) pension accounts	1.7	7.4	14.7	348%	98%	786%
Mean (DB) pension wealth	54.3	40.1	33.7	-26.1%	-16.1%	-38.0%
Mean Social Security wealth	151.0	70.0	91.9	-53.6%	31.2%	-39.1%
Mean retirement wealth	207.0	117.6	140.2	-43.2%	19.2%	-32.3%
Mean augmented wealth	322.0	290.1	217.5	-9.9%	-25.0%	-32.5%
3. Age: 65-70						
Mean income	22.9	19.9	26.5	-13.2%	33.0%	15.4%
Mean net worth (HDW)	121.9	157.0	118.1	28.8%	-24.8%	-3.1%
Mean financial wealth	63.8	106.4	59.5	66.9%	-44.0%	-6.6%
Mean home equity	58.2	50.7	58.6	-12.9%	15.6%	0.7%
Mean (DC) pension accounts	1.2	1.2	6.6	3%	428%	444%
Mean (DB) pension wealth	50.4	65.3	37.9	29.7%	-42.0%	-24.8%
Mean Social Security wealth	153.9	96.5	109.6	-37.3%	13.5%	-28.8%
Mean retirement wealth	205.5	163.1	154.0	-20.6%	-5.6%	-25.0%
Mean augmented wealth	326.2	318.9	265.5	-2.2%	-16.7%	-18.6%
4. Age: 71 and over						
Mean income	15.0	19.9	16.7	32.2%	-16.0%	11.1%
Mean net worth (HDW)	107.3	158.3	112.3	47.6%	-29.1%	4.6%
Mean financial wealth	67.5	99.8	58.2	47.9%	-41.7%	-13.8%
Mean home equity	39.8	58.6	54.1	47.0%	-7.6%	35.8%
Mean (DC) pension accounts	0.1	0.0	3.0	-86%	—	2598%
Mean (DB) pension wealth	34.0	61.8	31.6	81.9%	-48.9%	-7.1%
Mean Social Security wealth	95.5	116.5	87.2	22.0%	-25.1%	-8.7%
Mean retirement wealth	129.6	178.3	121.9	37.6%	-31.7%	-6.0%
Mean augmented wealth	236.8	336.6	231.1	42.2%	-31.4%	-2.4%

Note: Households are classified by the age of the head of household and the schooling level of the head of household.

Key:
1. Retirement wealth = DC pension accounts + gross DB pension wealth + Social Security wealth.
2. Augmented wealth = net worth + retirement wealth.

Source: Author's computations from the 1983, 1989, and 1998 Survey of Consumer Finances.

APPENDIX TABLE 13 (PART 2 OF 4)
Household income and wealth by education and age class, 1983-98
(in thousands, 1998 dollars)

| | 1983 | 1989 | 1998 | Percentage change | | |
				1983-89	1989-98	1983-98
B. 12 years of schooling						
1. Age: 53-58						
Mean income	$49.3	$49.7	$39.2	0.9%	-21.2%	-20.5%
Mean net worth (HDW)	251.7	246.3	147.5	-2.1%	-40.1%	-41.4%
Mean financial wealth	174.8	167.1	90.8	-4.4%	-45.7%	-48.1%
Mean home equity	76.9	79.2	56.7	3.0%	-28.3%	-26.2%
Mean (DC) pension accounts	4.8	11.0	29.2	130%	165%	508%
Mean (DB) pension wealth	87.5	39.1	41.7	-55.3%	6.7%	-52.4%
Mean Social Security wealth	149.9	95.1	139.1	-36.5%	46.3%	-7.2%
Mean retirement wealth	242.2	145.2	210.1	-40.0%	44.7%	-13.3%
Mean augmented wealth	489.1	380.5	328.4	-22.2%	-13.7%	-32.9%
2. Age: 59-64						
Mean income	39.2	48.9	41.6	24.8%	-14.9%	6.2%
Mean net worth (HDW)	242.3	385.0	300.6	58.9%	-21.9%	24.1%
Mean financial wealth	165.2	290.9	223.5	76.0%	-23.2%	35.2%
Mean home equity	77.0	94.1	77.2	22.1%	-18.0%	0.2%
Mean (DC) pension accounts	2.7	6.7	42.6	144%	536%	1452%
Mean (DB) pension wealth	84.2	54.6	70.4	-35.1%	28.8%	-16.4%
Mean Social Security wealth	181.6	124.4	155.1	-31.5%	24.6%	-14.6%
Mean retirement wealth	268.5	185.8	268.1	-30.8%	44.3%	-0.2%
Mean augmented wealth	508.1	564.0	526.1	11.0%	-6.7%	3.6%
3. Age: 65-70						
Mean income	35.7	30.8	35.3	-13.5%	14.6%	-0.9%
Mean net worth (HDW)	304.0	350.8	272.2	15.4%	-22.4%	-10.4%
Mean financial wealth	219.0	256.8	173.9	17.3%	-32.3%	-20.6%
Mean home equity	85.0	94.0	98.3	10.6%	4.6%	15.7%
Mean (DC) pension accounts	0.1	0.1	31.3	46%	—	—
Mean (DB) pension wealth	66.9	120.5	61.9	80.3%	-48.7%	-7.5%
Mean Social Security wealth	184.2	152.0	175.7	-17.5%	15.6%	-4.6%
Mean retirement wealth	251.1	272.6	268.8	8.6%	-1.4%	7.1%
Mean augmented wealth	555.0	623.3	509.8	12.3%	-18.2%	-8.2%
4. Age: 71 & over						
Mean income	30.7	38.5	29.2	25.5%	-24.2%	-4.9%
Mean net worth (HDW)	276.3	458.2	289.3	65.9%	-36.9%	4.7%
Mean financial wealth	207.3	350.2	201.8	68.9%	-42.4%	-2.7%
Mean home equity	69.0	108.0	87.5	56.7%	-19.0%	26.9%
Mean (DC) pension accounts	-	-	12.3	—	—	—
Mean (DB) pension wealth	56.4	139.9	53.0	148.3%	-62.1%	-5.9%
Mean Social Security wealth	127.3	177.7	101.3	39.5%	-43.0%	-20.4%
Mean retirement wealth	183.7	317.6	166.6	72.9%	-47.5%	-9.3%
Mean augmented wealth	460.0	775.8	443.7	68.7%	-42.8%	-3.5%

Note: Households are classified by the age of the head of household and the schooling level of the head of household.

Key:
1. Retirement wealth = DC pension accounts + gross DB pension wealth + Social Security wealth.
2. Augmented wealth = net worth + retirement wealth.

Source: Author's computations from the 1983, 1989, and 1998 Survey of Consumer Finances.

APPENDIX TABLE 13 (PART 3 OF 4)
Household income and wealth by education and age class, 1983-98
(in thousands, 1998 dollars)

	1983	1989	1998	Percentage change 1983-89	1989-98	1983-98
C. 13-15 years of schooling						
1. Age: 53-58						
Mean income	$64.2	$73.2	$70.0	14.0%	-4.4%	9.0%
Mean net worth (HDW)	386.2	370.1	351.6	-4.2%	-5.0%	-9.0%
Mean financial wealth	273.8	265.7	289.6	-3.0%	9.0%	5.8%
Mean home equity	112.3	104.4	61.9	-7.1%	-40.6%	-44.9%
Mean (DC) pension accounts	10.3	18.2	43.0	78%	136%	319%
Mean (DB) pension wealth	126.5	38.6	45.4	-69.5%	17.4%	-64.2%
Mean Social Security wealth	133.3	82.7	133.1	-38.0%	61.0%	-0.1%
Mean retirement wealth	270.1	139.6	221.5	-48.3%	58.7%	-18.0%
Mean augmented wealth	646.0	491.4	530.0	-23.9%	7.9%	-18.0%
2. Age: 59-64						
Mean income	79.9	76.6	57.2	-4.1%	-25.4%	-28.5%
Mean net worth (HDW)	706.6	498.5	470.8	-29.5%	-5.5%	-33.4%
Mean financial wealth	561.7	373.8	373.5	-33.4%	-0.1%	-33.5%
Mean home equity	144.9	124.6	97.3	-14.0%	-22.0%	-32.9%
Mean (DC) pension accounts	7.3	12.2	92.2	68%	656%	1170%
Mean (DB) pension wealth	139.3	52.4	82.5	-62.4%	57.5%	-40.8%
Mean Social Security wealth	182.4	117.4	190.6	-35.6%	62.3%	4.5%
Mean retirement wealth	329.0	182.0	365.4	-44.7%	100.7%	11.1%
Mean augmented wealth	1,028.3	668.3	743.9	-35.0%	11.3%	-27.7%
3. Age: 65-70						
Mean income	56.8	72.5	48.3	27.5%	-33.3%	-15.0%
Mean net worth (HDW)	556.7	1,164.6	466.2	109.2%	-60.0%	-16.3%
Mean financial wealth	444.8	1,051.6	341.8	136.4%	-67.5%	-23.2%
Mean home equity	111.9	113.0	124.4	0.9%	10.1%	11.1%
Mean (DC) pension accounts	4.6	9.6	46.3	108%	384%	908%
Mean (DB) pension wealth	66.0	144.7	98.2	119.1%	-32.2%	48.7%
Mean Social Security wealth	180.9	138.1	172.7	-23.7%	25.1%	-4.5%
Mean retirement wealth	251.5	292.4	317.2	16.3%	8.5%	26.1%
Mean augmented wealth	803.7	1,447.4	737.2	80.1%	-49.1%	-8.3%
4. Age: 71 and over						
Mean income	28.1	58.3	30.6	107.6%	-47.5%	8.9%
Mean net worth (HDW)	456.3	998.6	396.4	118.9%	-60.3%	-13.1%
Mean financial wealth	353.9	861.8	295.8	143.5%	-65.7%	-16.4%
Mean home equity	102.4	136.8	100.6	33.6%	-26.4%	-1.8%
Mean (DC) pension accounts	11.9	6.4	22.2	-46%	248%	87%
Mean (DB) pension wealth	42.0	150.1	63.8	257.7%	-57.5%	52.0%
Mean Social Security wealth	117.5	176.4	98.4	50.1%	-44.2%	-16.2%
Mean retirement wealth	171.3	332.9	184.4	94.3%	-44.6%	7.6%
Mean augmented wealth	615.7	1,325.1	558.6	115.2%	-57.8%	-9.3%

Note: Households are classified by the age of the head of household and the schooling level of the head of household.

Key:
1. Retirement wealth = DC pension accounts + gross DB pension wealth + Social Security wealth.
2. Augmented wealth = net worth + retirement wealth.

Source: Author's computations from the 1983, 1989, and 1998 Survey of Consumer Finances.

APPENDIX TABLE 13 (PART 4 OF 4)
Household income and wealth by education and age class, 1983-98
(in thousands, 1998 dollars)

	1983	1989	1998	Percentage change 1983-89	1989-98	1983-98
D. 16 or more years of schooling						
1. Age: 53-58						
Mean income	$112.9	$151.2	$138.7	33.9%	-8.3%	22.8%
Mean net worth (HDW)	741.2	1,160.1	999.8	56.5%	-13.8%	34.9%
Mean financial wealth	595.0	968.5	863.4	62.8%	-10.8%	45.1%
Mean home equity	146.2	191.7	136.4	31.1%	-28.8%	-6.7%
Mean (DC) pension accounts	22.3	68.6	153.0	207%	123%	585%
Mean (DB) pension wealth	156.1	69.5	79.5	-55.5%	14.5%	-49.0%
Mean Social Security wealth	156.4	117.6	137.5	-24.8%	16.9%	-12.1%
Mean retirement wealth	334.9	255.7	370.1	-23.6%	44.7%	10.5%
Mean augmented wealth	1,053.7	1,347.2	1,216.9	27.9%	-9.7%	15.5%
2. Age: 59-64						
Mean income	113.3	121.6	155.8	7.3%	28.2%	37.5%
Mean net worth (HDW)	811.5	1,152.6	1,451.4	42.0%	25.9%	78.9%
Mean financial wealth	640.5	952.9	1,254.3	48.8%	31.6%	95.8%
Mean home equity	171.0	199.7	197.1	16.8%	-1.3%	15.3%
Mean (DC) pension accounts	19.9	38.2	272.2	92%	612%	1270%
Mean (DB) pension wealth	177.9	112.0	158.5	-37.0%	41.5%	-10.9%
Mean Social Security wealth	207.4	153.3	163.7	-26.1%	6.8%	-21.1%
Mean retirement wealth	405.2	303.5	594.4	-25.1%	95.9%	46.7%
Mean augmented wealth	1,196.8	1,417.9	1,773.6	18.5%	25.1%	48.2%
3. Age: 65-70						
Mean income	125.3	148.8	91.1	18.7%	-38.8%	-27.3%
Mean net worth (HDW)	1,741.9	1,993.5	1,051.3	14.4%	-47.3%	-39.6%
Mean financial wealth	1,555.5	1,714.0	903.4	10.2%	-47.3%	-41.9%
Mean home equity	186.4	279.6	147.9	49.9%	-47.1%	-20.7%
Mean (DC) pension accounts	5.3	17.7	133.7	235%	656%	2435%
Mean (DB) pension wealth	164.7	244.6	211.3	48.5%	-13.6%	28.3%
Mean Social Security wealth	191.0	184.2	204.2	-3.6%	10.8%	6.9%
Mean retirement wealth	361.0	446.5	549.2	23.7%	23.0%	52.1%
Mean augmented wealth	2,097.6	2,422.3	1,466.7	15.5%	-39.4%	-30.1%
4. Age: 71 and over						
Mean income	83.2	100.0	63.7	20.2%	-36.3%	-23.4%
Mean net worth (HDW)	955.4	909.0	797.6	-4.9%	-12.3%	-16.5%
Mean financial wealth	833.1	741.1	639.8	-11.0%	-13.7%	-23.2%
Mean home equity	122.3	167.8	157.8	37.2%	-6.0%	29.0%
Mean (DC) pension accounts	2.0	5.6	69.5	180%	1149%	3396%
Mean (DB) pension wealth	95.0	397.0	140.0	318.1%	-64.7%	47.4%
Mean Social Security wealth	173.5	191.3	145.5	10.3%	-24.0%	-16.2%
Mean retirement wealth	270.5	593.9	355.0	119.6%	-40.2%	31.3%
Mean augmented wealth	1,223.9	1,497.3	1,083.0	22.3%	-27.7%	-11.5%

Note: Households are classified by the age of the head of household and the schooling level of the head of household.
Key:
1. Retirement wealth = DC pension accounts + gross DB pension wealth + Social Security wealth.
2. Augmented wealth = net worth + retirement wealth.

Source: Author's computations from the 1983, 1989, and 1998 Survey of Consumer Finances.

APPENDIX TABLE 14 (PART 1 OF 3)
Household income and wealth by family status and age class, 1983-89
(in thousands, 1998 dollars)

	1983	1989	1998	Percentage change 1983-89	1989-98	1983-98
A. Married couple						
1. Age: 53-58						
Mean income	$77.7	$78.2	$99.2	0.6%	26.9%	27.6%
Mean net worth (HDW)	467.8	470.2	609.5	0.5%	29.6%	30.3%
Mean financial wealth	349.3	361.1	506.5	3.4%	40.3%	45.0%
Mean home equity	118.5	109.1	103.0	-7.9%	-5.7%	-13.1%
Mean (DC) pension accounts	11.7	25.0	87.1	114%	249%	648%
Mean (DB) pension wealth	119.1	68.6	60.3	-42.4%	-12.1%	-49.4%
Mean Social Security wealth	182.9	123.7	165.1	-32.4%	33.5%	-9.7%
Mean retirement wealth	313.6	217.2	312.5	-30.7%	43.8%	-0.4%
Mean augmented wealth	769.7	662.4	834.8	-13.9%	26.0%	8.5%
2. Age: 59-64						
Mean income	68.4	69.9	90.8	2.3%	29.9%	32.8%
Mean net worth (HDW)	473.3	560.6	761.0	18.4%	35.7%	60.8%
Mean financial wealth	358.9	439.1	635.6	22.3%	44.7%	77.1%
Mean home equity	114.4	121.6	125.4	6.3%	3.2%	9.6%
Mean (DC) pension accounts	8.3	14.9	140.5	80%	843%	1597%
Mean (DB) pension wealth	109.8	152.3	108.4	38.7%	-28.8%	-1.3%
Mean Social Security wealth	227.3	162.3	188.1	-28.6%	15.9%	-17.2%
Mean retirement wealth	345.4	329.5	437.0	-4.6%	32.6%	26.5%
Mean augmented wealth	810.4	875.2	1,057.5	8.0%	20.8%	30.5%
3. Age: 65-70						
Mean income	60.2	57.0	69.9	-5.3%	22.5%	16.1%
Mean net worth (HDW)	625.8	709.6	653.7	13.4%	-7.9%	4.5%
Mean financial wealth	518.6	589.0	514.0	13.6%	-12.7%	-0.9%
Mean home equity	107.2	120.6	139.7	12.5%	15.8%	30.4%
Mean (DC) pension accounts	3.1	5.4	74.5	77%	1276%	2330%
Mean (DB) pension wealth	70.8	167.6	128.0	136.6%	-23.6%	80.8%
Mean Social Security wealth	232.5	178.1	211.0	-23.4%	18.4%	-9.2%
Mean retirement wealth	306.3	351.1	413.5	14.6%	17.8%	35.0%
Mean augmented wealth	929.1	1,055.3	992.7	13.6%	-5.9%	6.9%
4. Age: 71 and over						
Mean income	38.6	49.5	46.2	28.1%	-6.6%	19.6%
Mean net worth (HDW)	387.7	508.1	494.5	31.0%	-2.7%	27.5%
Mean financial wealth	308.9	396.0	369.1	28.2%	-6.8%	19.5%
Mean home equity	78.8	112.1	125.4	42.3%	11.9%	59.2%
Mean (DC) pension accounts	3.2	2.1	41.9	-34%	1855%	1196%
Mean (DB) pension wealth	44.3	77.1	92.6	74.0%	20.2%	109.1%
Mean Social Security wealth	198.1	151.9	150.6	-23.3%	-0.9%	-24.0%
Mean retirement wealth	245.6	231.1	285.1	-5.9%	23.4%	16.1%
Mean augmented wealth	630.1	737.1	737.7	17.0%	0.1%	17.1%

Note: Households are classified by the age of the head of household.
Key:
1. Retirement wealth = DC pension accounts + gross DB pension wealth + Social Security wealth.
2. Augmented wealth = net worth (HDW) + retirement wealth.

Source: Author's computations from the 1983, 1989, and 1998 Survey of Consumer Finances.

APPENDIX TABLE 14 (PART 2 OF 3)
Household income and wealth by family status and age class, 1983-89
(in thousands, 1998 dollars)

	1983	1989	1998	Percentage change		
				1983-89	1989-98	1983-98
B. Single male						
1. Age: 53-58						
Mean income	$42.7	$39.6	$49.1	-7.2%	23.9%	15.0%
Mean net worth (HDW)	265.9	228.9	312.6	-13.9%	36.6%	17.6%
Mean financial wealth	225.5	184.5	270.9	-18.2%	46.8%	20.2%
Mean home equity	40.4	44.3	41.7	9.6%	-6.0%	3.1%
Mean (DC) pension accounts	1.6	14.2	60.0	794%	321%	3665%
Mean (DB) pension wealth	23.9	34.1	49.1	42.5%	44.0%	105.2%
Mean Social Security wealth	78.4	49.0	67.1	-37.5%	36.9%	-14.4%
Mean retirement wealth	103.9	97.3	176.2	-6.3%	81.0%	69.5%
Mean augmented wealth	368.2	311.9	428.8	-15.3%	37.4%	16.4%
2. Age: 59-64						
Mean income	28.0	33.6	56.5	20.2%	68.0%	101.9%
Mean net worth (HDW)	175.1	192.0	422.3	9.7%	120.0%	141.2%
Mean financial wealth	109.7	120.9	338.5	10.2%	180.0%	208.6%
Mean home equity	65.4	71.1	83.7	8.7%	17.8%	28.1%
Mean (DC) pension accounts	—	4.3	69.6	—	1508%	—
Mean (DB) pension wealth	65.3	64.9	54.2	-0.6%	-16.5%	-17.0%
Mean Social Security wealth	82.4	61.3	83.8	-25.6%	36.8%	1.7%
Mean retirement wealth	147.8	130.5	207.7	-11.7%	59.1%	40.6%
Mean augmented wealth	322.8	318.2	560.3	-1.4%	76.1%	73.6%
3. Age: 65-70						
Mean income	26.4	21.5	35.1	-18.6%	63.3%	32.9%
Mean net worth (HDW)	231.9	233.5	361.2	0.7%	54.7%	55.8%
Mean financial wealth	169.5	193.8	293.8	14.3%	51.6%	73.3%
Mean home equity	62.4	39.7	67.5	-36.3%	69.8%	8.2%
Mean (DC) pension accounts	—	—	49.9	—	—	—
Mean (DB) pension wealth	58.9	91.7	70.9	55.6%	-22.7%	20.3%
Mean Social Security wealth	90.7	78.4	131.1	-13.6%	67.3%	44.6%
Mean retirement wealth	149.6	170.0	251.9	13.7%	48.1%	68.4%
Mean augmented wealth	381.5	403.6	563.2	5.8%	39.6%	47.6%
4. Age: 71 and over						
Mean income	25.3	21.5	28.0	-15.1%	29.9%	10.3%
Mean net worth (HDW)	185.7	115.7	454.4	-37.7%	292.7%	144.7%
Mean financial wealth	147.9	80.5	393.7	-45.6%	389.2%	166.1%
Mean home equity	37.8	35.2	60.7	-6.8%	72.4%	60.7%
Mean (DC) pension accounts	—	—	16.9	—	—	—
Mean (DB) pension wealth	31.0	27.9	36.2	-10.0%	29.6%	16.7%
Mean Social Security wealth	63.9	62.6	72.8	-2.0%	16.3%	13.9%
Mean retirement wealth	95.0	90.6	126.0	-4.6%	39.1%	32.7%
Mean augmented wealth	280.7	206.3	563.4	-26.5%	173.1%	100.7%

Note: Households are classified by the age of the head of household.
Key:
1. Retirement wealth = DC pension accounts + gross DB pension wealth + Social Security wealth.
2. Augmented wealth = net worth (HDW) + retirement wealth.

Source: Author's computations from the 1983, 1989, and 1998 Survey of Consumer Finances.

APPENDIX TABLE 14 (PART 3 OF 3)
Household income and wealth by family status and age class, 1983-89
(in thousands, 1998 dollars)

	1983	1989	1998	Percentage change 1983-89	1989-98	1983-98
C.Single female						
1. Age: 53-58						
Mean income	$35.7	$25.2	$29.2	-29.3%	15.8%	-18.1%
Mean net worth (HDW)	148.3	116.9	147.4	-21.1%	26.0%	-0.6%
Mean financial wealth	103.7	56.1	105.0	-45.9%	87.3%	1.3%
Mean home equity	44.6	60.9	42.3	36.4%	-30.4%	-5.1%
Mean (DC) pension accounts	4.5	2.1	21.2	-53%	902%	375%
Mean (DB) pension wealth	66.5	37.8	29.2	-43.1%	-22.8%	-56.1%
Mean Social Security wealth	62.0	54.4	56.7	-12.3%	4.3%	-8.5%
Mean retirement wealth	132.9	94.3	107.1	-29.1%	13.6%	-19.4%
Mean augmented wealth	276.7	209.1	233.3	-24.4%	11.6%	-15.7%
2. Age: 59-64						
Mean income	21.8	23.8	23.9	9.2%	0.5%	9.8%
Mean net worth (HDW)	123.7	196.9	231.0	59.2%	17.4%	86.8%
Mean financial wealth	71.8	132.3	168.9	84.3%	27.7%	135.2%
Mean home equity	51.9	64.6	62.2	24.4%	-3.8%	19.8%
Mean (DC) pension accounts	1.6	13.3	34.2	754%	158%	2102%
Mean (DB) pension wealth	70.3	52.8	54.5	-24.9%	3.4%	-22.4%
Mean Social Security wealth	65.7	62.6	91.5	-4.7%	46.1%	39.2%
Mean retirement wealth	137.5	128.7	180.2	-6.5%	40.1%	31.0%
Mean augmented wealth	259.7	312.3	377.0	20.2%	20.7%	45.2%
3. Age: 65-70						
Mean income	22.2	19.1	20.1	-14.1%	5.2%	-9.6%
Mean net worth (HDW)	200.2	155.9	189.7	-22.1%	21.6%	-5.3%
Mean financial wealth	134.5	101.7	129.9	-24.4%	27.8%	-3.5%
Mean home equity	65.7	54.3	59.8	-17.4%	10.2%	-9.0%
Mean (DC) pension accounts	0.1	1.3	21.2	1233%	1550%	21896%
Mean (DB) pension wealth	78.6	57.3	63.9	-27.1%	11.6%	-18.7%
Mean Social Security wealth	69.9	102.7	99.3	47.0%	-3.4%	42.0%
Mean retirement wealth	148.5	161.3	184.4	8.6%	14.3%	24.1%
Mean augmented wealth	348.6	315.9	352.8	-9.4%	11.7%	1.2%
4. Age: 71 and over						
Mean income	15.8	18.4	18.8	16.4%	2.0%	18.8%
Mean net worth (HDW)	152.9	160.6	168.0	5.1%	4.6%	9.9%
Mean financial wealth	108.3	104.1	101.7	-3.9%	-2.3%	-6.1%
Mean home equity	44.6	56.6	66.3	26.8%	17.2%	48.7%
Mean (DC) pension accounts	0.0	—	3.4	—	—	—
Mean (DB) pension wealth	45.7	30.7	42.6	-32.9%	39.0%	-6.7%
Mean Social Security wealth	45.3	85.0	69.4	87.5%	-18.3%	53.2%
Mean retirement wealth	91.0	115.6	115.5	27.0%	-0.2%	26.9%
Mean augmented wealth	243.9	276.3	280.1	13.3%	1.4%	14.8%

Note: Households are classified by the age of the head of household.
Key:
1. Retirement wealth = DC pension accounts + gross DB pension wealth + Social Security wealth.
2. Augmented wealth = net worth (HDW) + retirement wealth.

Source: Author's computations from the 1983, 1989, and 1998 Survey of Consumer Finances.

APPENDIX TABLE 15 (PART 1 OF 2)
Household income and wealth by homeowner status and age class, 1983-98
(in thousands, 1998 dollars)

	1983	1989	1998	Percentage change 1983-89	1989-98	1983-98
A. Homeowner						
1. Age: 53-58						
Mean income	$71.8	$68.3	$85.9	-4.9%	25.8%	19.7%
Mean net worth (HDW)	450.6	421.4	560.6	-6.5%	33.0%	24.4%
Mean financial wealth	330.1	309.8	459.3	-6.2%	48.3%	39.1%
Mean home equity	120.4	111.7	101.3	-7.3%	-9.3%	-15.9%
Mean (DC) pension accounts	10.7	21.4	79.5	100%	271%	645%
Mean (DB) pension wealth	109.1	56.2	54.7	-48.6%	-2.6%	-49.9%
Mean Social Security wealth	156.0	105.3	131.7	-32.5%	25.0%	-15.6%
Mean retirement wealth	275.8	182.9	265.9	-33.7%	45.4%	-3.6%
Mean augmented wealth	715.7	582.9	747.0	-18.6%	28.2%	4.4%
2. Age: 59-64						
Mean income	60.9	60.1	80.1	-1.2%	33.2%	31.6%
Mean net worth (HDW)	439.6	507.9	696.4	15.5%	37.1%	58.4%
Mean financial wealth	321.6	381.2	569.5	18.5%	49.4%	77.1%
Mean home equity	118.1	126.7	126.8	7.3%	0.1%	7.4%
Mean (DC) pension accounts	7.3	15.3	121.1	109%	689%	1549%
Mean (DB) pension wealth	108.0	64.1	98.3	-40.7%	53.4%	-9.0%
Mean Social Security wealth	186.0	111.0	162.7	-40.3%	46.6%	-12.5%
Mean retirement wealth	301.3	190.4	382.1	-36.8%	100.6%	26.8%
Mean augmented wealth	733.6	683.0	957.4	-6.9%	40.2%	30.5%
3. Age: 65-70						
Mean income	50.5	43.0	57.3	-14.9%	33.3%	13.3%
Mean net worth (HDW)	541.5	520.1	567.1	-3.9%	9.0%	4.7%
Mean financial wealth	429.1	408.1	437.3	-4.9%	7.2%	1.9%
Mean home equity	112.4	112.1	129.8	-0.3%	15.8%	15.5%
Mean (DC) pension accounts	2.4	3.5	63.9	48%	1707%	2573%
Mean (DB) pension wealth	77.4	134.0	116.7	73.1%	-12.9%	50.8%
Mean Social Security wealth	177.2	137.0	177.3	-22.7%	29.5%	0.0%
Mean retirement wealth	257.0	274.4	357.8	6.8%	30.4%	39.2%
Mean augmented wealth	796.1	791.1	861.0	-0.6%	8.8%	8.2%
4. Age: 71 and over						
Mean income	29.8	37.1	35.0	24.1%	-5.6%	17.2%
Mean net worth (HDW)	325.3	387.4	401.3	19.1%	3.6%	23.4%
Mean financial wealth	241.8	279.6	285.4	15.6%	2.1%	18.1%
Mean home equity	83.5	107.8	115.9	29.1%	7.5%	38.7%
Mean (DC) pension accounts	1.9	0.7	23.0	-62%	3013%	1084%
Mean (DB) pension wealth	48.8	128.6	71.8	163.6%	-44.2%	47.1%
Mean Social Security wealth	120.3	154.5	111.2	28.5%	-28.0%	-7.5%
Mean retirement wealth	171.0	283.8	205.9	66.0%	-27.4%	20.4%
Mean augmented wealth	494.4	670.5	584.3	35.6%	-12.9%	18.2%

Note: Households are classified by the age of the head of household.
Key:
1. Retirement wealth = DC pension accounts + gross DB pension wealth + Social Security wealth.
2. Augmented wealth = net worth (HDW) + retirement wealth.

Source: Author's computations from the 1983, 1989, and 1998 Survey of Consumer Finances.

APPENDIX TABLE 15 (PART 2 OF 2)
Household income and wealth by homeowner status and age class, 1983-98
(in thousands, 1998 dollars)

	1983	1989	1998	Percentage change		
				1983-89	1989-98	1983-98
B. Renter						
1. Age: 53-58						
Mean income	$33.7	$26.0	$32.0	-23.0%	23.0%	-5.3%
Mean net worth (HDW)	63.1	56.0	47.4	-11.3%	-15.4%	-25.0%
Mean financial wealth	63.1	59.2	47.4	-6.2%	-20.0%	-25.0%
Mean home equity	—	—	—	—	—	—
Mean (DC) pension accounts	3.1	2.5	17.7	-21%	615%	468%
Mean (DB) pension wealth	60.0	14.0	35.3	-76.6%	151.7%	-41.1%
Mean Social Security wealth	85.7	55.5	94.9	-35.3%	71.1%	10.7%
Mean retirement wealth	148.8	72.0	147.9	-51.6%	105.5%	-0.6%
Mean augmented wealth	208.9	125.5	177.6	-39.9%	41.5%	-15.0%
2. Age: 59-64						
Mean income	22.6	22.4	20.9	-1.0%	-6.7%	-7.6%
Mean net worth (HDW)	42.4	43.4	70.0	2.3%	61.3%	65.1%
Mean financial wealth	42.4	44.3	70.0	4.6%	57.9%	65.1%
Mean home equity	—	—	—	—	—	—
Mean (DC) pension accounts	0.8	4.0	29.8	420%	639%	3741%
Mean (DB) pension wealth	50.7	26.6	41.4	-47.5%	55.7%	-18.3%
Mean Social Security wealth	128.0	65.4	97.0	-48.9%	48.3%	-24.2%
Mean retirement wealth	179.4	96.0	168.2	-46.5%	75.2%	-6.2%
Mean augmented wealth	221.1	135.4	208.4	-38.8%	53.9%	-5.7%
3. Age: 65-70						
Mean income	25.7	21.6	17.3	-15.8%	-19.9%	-32.6%
Mean net worth (HDW)	134.3	162.8	43.1	21.2%	-73.6%	-68.0%
Mean financial wealth	134.3	163.7	43.1	21.9%	-73.7%	-68.0%
Mean home equity	—	(0.9)	—	—	—	—
Mean (DC) pension accounts	—	2.0	12.2	—	—	—
Mean (DB) pension wealth	56.9	33.8	31.3	-40.6%	-7.3%	-45.0%
Mean Social Security wealth	145.8	78.8	115.7	-45.9%	46.8%	-20.6%
Mean retirement wealth	202.7	114.6	159.2	-43.4%	38.9%	-21.5%
Mean augmented wealth	337.1	275.5	190.1	-18.3%	-31.0%	-43.6%
4. Age: 71 and over						
Mean income	16.0	19.4	18.0	21.6%	-7.6%	12.4%
Mean net worth (HDW)	82.0	94.3	101.9	15.0%	8.1%	24.2%
Mean financial wealth	82.0	94.3	101.9	15.0%	8.1%	24.2%
Mean home equity	—	—	—	—	—	—
Mean (DC) pension accounts	0.0	1.5	13.9	5326%	833%	50530%
Mean (DB) pension wealth	35.0	71.1	31.7	103.3%	-55.4%	-9.2%
Mean Social Security wealth	88.4	88.0	78.3	-0.5%	-11.0%	-11.5%
Mean retirement wealth	123.4	160.6	123.9	30.1%	-22.8%	0.4%
Mean augmented wealth	205.4	253.4	211.9	23.4%	-16.4%	3.2%

Note: Households are classified by the age of the head of household.
Key:
1. Retirement wealth = DC pension accounts + gross DB pension wealth + Social Security wealth.
2. Augmented wealth = net worth (HDW) + retirement wealth.

Source: Author's computations from the 1983, 1989, and 1998 Survey of Consumer Finances.

Endnotes

1.   African Americans are combined with Hispanics in order to maintain adequate sample sizes by age group.

2.   Comparable data on future pension benefits are not available in the 1983 Survey of Consumer Finances.

3.   The relative income preparedness of racial groups found here is consistent with the Moore and Mitchell (2000) study.

4.   Bernheim (1997) also found higher income adequacy for married couples in comparison to single male and female households.

5.   These results accord well with those calculated by Bernheim (1997) on the basis of private wealth holdings alone. Moreover, these findings of very low replacement rates are comparable to those of Gustman and Steinmeier (1998), who used the 1992 Health and Retirement Study, and to those of Engen, Gale, and Uccello (1999), who used both the 1992 wave of the HRS and the 1983, 1992, and 1995 Survey of Consumer Finances.

6.   Technically speaking, the mortality rate m_t associated with the year of retirement is the probability of surviving from the current age to the age of retirement.

7.   Separate imputations are performed for husband and wife, and an adjustment in the Social Security benefit is made for the surviving spouse.

8.   As with pension wealth, the mortality rate mt associated with the year of retirement is the probability of surviving from the current age to the age of retirement.

9.   A third though minor component is also provided: pensions from other non-specified sources.

10.   This implicitly assumes that deviations from the regression line in the current year are a result of a transitory component to current income only. This procedure follows the conventions of the 1983 SCF codebook.

References

Bernheim, D.B. 1997. "The Adequacy of Personal Retirement Saving: Issues and Options." In David A. Wise, ed., *Facing the Age Wave.* Stanford, Calif.: Hoover Institute Press.

Bloom, David E., and Richard B. Freeman. 1992. "The Fall in Private Pension Coverage in the United States." *American Economic Review Papers and Proceedings* 82(2): 539-58.

Chernick, Howard, and Edward N. Wolff. 1996. "The Distributional Effects of Raising the Social Security Retirement Age and Partially Indexing Social Security Benefits." Working Paper No. 115. Washington, D.C.: Economic Policy Institute.

Engen, E.M., W.G. Gale, and C.E. Uccello. 1999. "The Adequacy of Household Saving." *Brookings Papers on Economic Activity* 2: 65-165.

Even, William E., and David A. Macpherson. 1994a. "Trends in Individual and Household Pension Coverage." Mimeo.

Even, William E., and David A. Macpherson. 1994b. "Why Did Male Pension Coverage Decline in the 1980s?" *Industrial and Labor Relations Review* 47(3): 429-53.

Even, William E., and David A. Macpherson. 1994c. "Why Has the Decline in Pension Coverage Accelerated Among Less Educated Workers?" Mimeo.

Even, William E., and David A. Macpherson. 1994d. "Gender Differences in Pensions." *Journal of Human Resources* 29(2): 555-87.

Feldstein, Martin S. 1974. "Social Security, Induced Retirement and Aggregate Capital Accumulation." *Journal of Political Economy* 82 (October): 905-26.

Feldstein, Martin S. 1976. "Social Security and the Distribution of Wealth." *Journal of the American Statistical Association* 71 (December): 800-7.

Gustman, Alan L., Olivia S. Mitchell, Andrew A. Samwick, and Thomas L. Steinmeier. 1997. "Pension and Social Security Wealth in the Health and Retirement Study." Working Paper No. W5912. Cambridge, Mass.: National Bureau of Economic Research.

Gustman, Alan L., and Thomas L. Steinmeier. 1998. "Effects of Pensions on Saving: Analysis With Data From the Health and Retirement Study." Working Paper No. W6681. Cambridge, Mass.: National Bureau of Economic Research.

Hurd, Michael. 1994. "The Economic Status of the Elderly in the United States." In Yukio Noguchi and David A. Wise, eds., *Aging in the United States and Japan.* Chicago, Ill.: University of Chicago Press, pp. 63-83.

Kennickell, Arthur B., and Annika E. Sunden. 1999. "Pensions, Social Security, and the Distribution of Wealth." Mimeo, Federal Reserve Board, Washington, D.C.

Kotlikoff, Laurence J., and Daniel E. Smith. 1983. *Pensions in the American Economy.* Chicago, Ill.: University of Chicago Press.

Modigliani, Franco, and Richard Brumberg. 1954. "Utility Analysis and the Consumption Function: An Interpretation of Cross-Section Data." In K. Kurihara, ed., *Post-Keynesian Economics.* New Brunswick, N.J.: Rutgers University Press.

Moore, James F., and Olivia S. Mitchell. 2000. "Projected Retirement Wealth and Saving Adequacy." In O. Mitchell, B. Hammond, and A. Rappaport, eds., *Forecasting Retirement Needs and Retirement Wealth.* Philadelphia, Pa.: University of Pennsylvania Press.

Popke, Leslie E. 1999. "Are 401(k) Plans Replacing Other Employer-Provided Pensions?" *Journal of Human Resources* 34(2): 346-68.

Poterba, James M., Steven F. Venti, and David A. Wise. 1998. "401(k) Plans and Future Patterns of Retirement Saving." *American Economic Review Papers and Proceedings* 88(2): 179-84.

Smith, James P. 1997. "The Changing Economic Circumstances of the Elderly: Income, Wealth, and Social Security." Public Policy Brief No. 8. Syracuse, N.Y.: Syracuse University

Venti, Steven F., and David A. Wise. 1998. "The Cause of Wealth Dispersion at Retirement: Choice or Chance?" *American Economic Review Papers and Proceedings* 88(2): 185-91.

U.S. Bureau of the Census. 1990. *Measuring the Effect of Benefits and Taxes on Income and Poverty: 1989.* Current Population Reports, Series P-60. No. 169-RD. Washington, D.C.: U.S. Government Printing Office.

U.S. Department of Labor, Pension and Welfare Benefits Administration. 2000. "Coverage Status of Workers Under Employer Provided Pension Plans: Findings From the Contingent Work Supplement to the February 1999 Current Population Survey." Washington D.C.: Department of Labor.

Wolff, Edward N. 1987. "The Effects of Pensions and Social Security on the Distribution of Wealth in the U.S." In E. Wolff, ed., *International Comparisons of Household Wealth Distribution.* Oxford, England: Oxford University Press.

Wolff, Edward N. 1988. "Social Security, Pensions, and the Life Cycle Accumulation of Wealth: Some Empirical Tests." *Annales d'Economie et de Statistique*, No. 9, Janvier/Mars.

Wolff, Edward N. 1990. "Wealth Holdings and Poverty Status in the United States." *Review of Income and Wealth* 36(2): 143-65.

Wolff, Edward N. 1992. "Methodological Issues in the Estimation of Retirement Wealth." In Daniel J. Slottje, ed., *Research in Economic Inequality.* Vol. 2. JAI Press, pp. 31-56.

Wolff, Edward N. 1993a. "Social Security Annuities and Transfers: Distributional and Tax Implications." In Dimitri B. Papadimitriou and Edward N. Wolff, eds., *Poverty and Prosperity in the USA in the Late Twentieth Century.* Macmillan, pp. 211-39.

Wolff, Edward N. 1993b. "The Distributional Implications of Social Security Annuities and Transfers on Household Wealth and Income." In E. Wolff, ed., *Research in Economic Inequality.* Vol. 4. JAI Press, pp. 131-57.

Wolff, Edward N. 2001. "Recent Trends in Wealth Ownership, From 1983 to 1998." In Thomas M. Shapiro and Edward N. Wolff, eds., *Assets for the Poor: The Benefits of Spreading Asset Ownership.* Russell Sage Press, pp. 34-73.

About EPI

The Economic Policy Institute was founded in 1986 to widen the debate about policies to achieve healthy economic growth, prosperity, and opportunity.

Today, despite recent rapid growth in the U.S. economy, inequality in wealth, wages, and income remains historically high. Expanding global competition, changes in the nature of work, and rapid technological advances are altering economic reality. Yet many of our policies, attitudes, and institutions are based on assumptions that no longer reflect real world conditions.

With the support of leaders from labor, business, and the foundation world, the Institute has sponsored research and public discussion of a wide variety of topics: trade and fiscal policies; trends in wages, incomes, and prices; the causes of the productivity slowdown; labor-market problems; rural and urban policies; inflation; state-level economic development strategies; comparative international economic performance; and studies of the overall health of the U.S. manufacturing sector and of specific key industries.

The Institute works with a growing network of innovative economists and other social science researchers in universities and research centers all over the country who are willing to go beyond the conventional wisdom in considering strategies for public policy.

Founding scholars of the Institute include Jeff Faux, EPI president; Lester Thurow, Sloan School of Management, MIT; Ray Marshall, former U.S. secretary of labor, professor at the LBJ School of Public Affairs, University of Texas; Barry Bluestone, Northeastern University; Robert Reich, former U.S. secretary of labor; and Robert Kuttner, author, editor of *The American Prospect,* and columnist for *Business Week* and the Washington Post Writers Group.

For additional information about the Institute, contact EPI at 1660 L Street, NW, Suite 1200, Washington, DC 20036, (202) 775-8810, or visit www.epinet.org.